RIDING *the* WAVE

Teacher Strategies for Navigating Change and Strengthening Key Relationships

JEREMY S. ADAMS

Solution Tree | Press

Copyright © 2020 by Solution Tree Press

Materials appearing here are copyrighted. With one exception, all rights are reserved. Readers may reproduce only those pages marked "Reproducible." Otherwise, no part of this book may be reproduced or transmitted in any form or by any means (electronic, photocopying, recording, or otherwise) without prior written permission of the publisher.

555 North Morton Street
Bloomington, IN 47404
800.733.6786 (toll free) / 812.336.7700
FAX: 812.336.7790

email: info@SolutionTree.com
SolutionTree.com

Visit **go.SolutionTree.com/teacherefficacy** to download the free reproducibles in this book.

Printed in the United States of America

Library of Congress Cataloging-in-Publication Data

Names: Adams, Jeremy S., 1976- author.
Title: Riding the wave : teacher strategies for navigating change and strengthening key relationships / Jeremy S. Adams.
Other titles: Teacher strategies for navigating change and strengthening key relationships
Description: Bloomington, Indiana : Solution Tree Press, 2020. | Includes bibliographical references and index.
Identifiers: LCCN 2019044271 (print) | LCCN 2019044272 (ebook) | ISBN 9781949539592 (Paperback) | ISBN 9781949539608 (eBook)
Subjects: LCSH: Effective teaching. | Teacher effectiveness. | Teachers--Professional relationships--United States. | Teacher-student relationships.
Classification: LCC LB1025.3 .A374 2020 (print) | LCC LB1025.3 (ebook) | DDC 371.102--dc23
LC record available at https://lccn.loc.gov/2019044271
LC ebook record available at https://lccn.loc.gov/2019044272

Solution Tree
Jeffrey C. Jones, CEO
Edmund M. Ackerman, President

Solution Tree Press
President and Publisher: Douglas M. Rife
Associate Publisher: Sarah Payne-Mills
Art Director: Rian Anderson
Managing Production Editor: Kendra Slayton
Production Editor: Rita Carlberg
Content Development Specialist: Amy Rubenstein
Copy Editor: Jessi Finn
Text and Cover Designer: Abigail Bowen
Editorial Assistant and Proofreader: Sarah Ludwig

To my wife, Jennifer

ACKNOWLEDGMENTS

I am frequently struck when reading the biographies of famous writers how often they write in isolation, deliberately distanced from both kin and community. This book, however, required the support, contributions, and assistance of countless friends, colleagues, and community members.

The idea for this book was hatched, of all places, in the parking lot of the high school where I teach, in the midst of a conversation with my best friend in the world, Craig Holliday. He has the unfortunate distinction of having read more of my writing than any other person. It would take me pages to thoroughly detail all his contributions to this project. I say in all honesty that he is a *Ride the Wave* maestro.

My friend and former principal, David Reese, has always believed in my dreams, both in the classroom and in the world of writing. I cannot recall him ever saying no to a request in our two decades of working together.

My friends at Bakersfield High School, specifically Kevin Reynier, Kristina Fierro, Don Ellsworth, Brett Bonetti, and Tom Sakowski, have always been positive and affirming witnesses to the peaks and valleys of my writing career. Without them, I never could have reached the zenith of having this book published. The current administration at Bakersfield High School has never been anything but warm and encouraging.

The long and serpentine path toward the publication of this book has had some significant signposts along the way that are worth mentioning. Thank you to Douglas Rife for promising me we would find a way to work together someday. I am thrilled it happened. Thank you to the extraordinary Amy Rubenstein, whose insights, mentorship, and, yes, friendship made this process a genuine joy to undertake. I have never encountered a more patient and committed professional in my days as either a teacher or a writer. Mega kudos also to Rita Carlberg, a maestro of organization, insight, and editing, whose sharp eyes and potent insights were nothing short of magical during a robust editorial process. Her work ethic leaves me in awe. Thank you to all the people at Solution Tree whose devotion to excellence and professional development is second to none.

Finally, thank you to my family, my students, and the entire Bakersfield community. My children and wife were endlessly patient with me as I wrote and researched for this manuscript. My brother Will is a constant source of encouragement, and my older brother, Howard, is a bottomless well of insights, quotes, and debates. Thank you to professional development gurus Jan Kenney of the Kern High School District and James Webb, formerly of the Hart Union High School District, for birthing ideas, reading rough drafts, and allowing me to pick their brains whenever it was necessary. Thank you to the students of the Bakersfield High School class of 2019 who were enthusiastic as they observed the book-writing process unfold in front of their very eyes in the second semester of their senior year. Sorry if I sometimes took too long grading your exams! An especially hearty thank-you to my fourth period teaching assistant, Kylie Caffee, who helped in numerous ways in regard to the organization of my research and the compilation of the bibliography.

Finally, my entire community—the local university where I teach, the local newspaper where I first discovered my writing voice, the local radio and television shows that frequently invite me on to talk about education issues, the local writing and education groups that promote my books and articles—has always encouraged my writing efforts. Not many writers know what it is like to have an entire community behind them. But I certainly do. I am a proud product of California's dusty but dynamic Central Valley. I hope this book is worthy of its efforts on my behalf.

Solution Tree Press would like to thank the following reviewers:

Erin Evans
Active Learning Leader
Cooley Elementary School
El Paso, Texas

Jeff Lahey
Assistant Principal
Flower Mound High School
Flower Mound, Texas

Teresa Haskiell
Mathematics Teacher
James Wood High School
Winchester, Virginia

Beth Maloney
Fifth-Grade Teacher
Sunset Hills Elementary School
Surprise, Arizona

Mark Janda
History Teacher
The Harker School
San Jose, California

Janet Reece
Spanish Teacher
Glenbard East High School
Lombard, Illinois

Acknowledgments

Lauren Smith
Instructional Coach
Noble Crossing Elementary
Noblesville, Indiana

Esther Wu
Language Arts Teacher
Mountain View High School
Mountain View, California

Visit **go.SolutionTree.com/teacherefficacy** to download the free reproducibles in this book.

TABLE *of* CONTENTS

About the Author xiii

Introduction 1
    Recognizing the Changes in Education 2
    Adapting to the Changes 3
    Strengthening Key Relationships 4
    Flourishing as an Educator 6
    Approaching the Book's Structure 8
    Recapturing the Magic 9

PART 1

The Self 11

Chapter 1
Recognizing the Need for Self-Care 13
    The Cumulative Toll of the 21st Century 14
    Teacher Stress and the Manifestations of Burnout 17
    The Benefits of Self-Care 19
    Summary 20

Chapter 2
Practicing Self-Care 23
    Strategy 1: Stay Yourself 23
    Strategy 2: Remember the Basics and Avoid Compassion Fatigue . . 24
    Strategy 3: Learn the Difference Between Good and Bad Coping . . 27

Strategy 4: Be Self-Reflective and Set Realistic Goals 29
Strategy 5: Optimize Optimism 32
Summary 35

PART 2

Students 37

Chapter 3
Understanding Stress Among the Desks 39

A Never-Ending To-Do List 40
Proliferating Platforms and the Problems They Breed 43
The Declining State of Student Mental Health 45
A Tightening Testing Regimen 47
The Violation of Perpetual School Violence 49
Summary 51

Chapter 4
Promoting Learning and Mitigating Student Anxiety 53

Strategy 1: Teach the Student, Not the Subject 53
Strategy 2: Find the Golden Mean of Technology Teaching 55
Strategy 3: Use Coping Strategies in the Classroom 59
Strategy 4: Relax by Standardizing Standardized Tests 62
Strategy 5: Aim for Pacified Teaching in a Violent Age 65
Summary 68

PART 3

Colleagues 71

Chapter 5
Unraveling the Conflict Among Teachers 73

The Echo in Teachers' Cafeterias 74
Generational Chasms in Professional Development 78

Jealousies and Juxtapositions in an Era of Accountability. 79

Good Friend, Poor Colleague or Good Colleague, Poor Friend. . . 82

Summary. 84

Chapter 6
Committing to Teacher Collaboration 85

Strategy 1: Create an Admirable Miniature Body Politic 85

Strategy 2: Seek Wise Mentors and Impressionable Mentees. 89

Strategy 3: Borrow, Tweak, and Share One Another's Ideas 91

Strategy 4: Show Up for Your Colleagues 95

Strategy 5: Cultivate Bottom-Up Collaboration. 96

Summary. 99

PART 4

Administration 103

Chapter 7
Identifying Divergent Teacher and Principal Perspectives 105

The Ultimate Position of Powerlessness 106

The Local and the Global 108

Ignored Voices, Hurt Feelings. 111

Threats to a Positive and Professional Climate 113

Summary. 115

Chapter 8
Maintaining Staff Cohesion Through Communication. 117

Strategy 1: Don't Play the Power Game 117

Strategy 2: Welcome and Offer Feedback and Reflection. 120

Strategy 3: Transform Through Transparency 123

Strategy 4: Employ Empathy, Not Sympathy, and
  Stop Administrator Stereotypes. 126

Summary. 128

PART 5

The Community 131

Chapter 9
Viewing Education From a Distance 133
    The Weight of the World 134
    High-Profile Shortcomings and Underreported Strengths 136
    The Myth of Systemic Educational Failure 139
    Summary 141

Chapter 10
Connecting Citizens and Schools 143
    Strategy 1: Highlight Successes 143
    Strategy 2: Look in the Rearview Mirror 147
    Strategy 3: Demonstrate Democracy 150
    Summary 154

Epilogue 157

References and Resources 161

Index 175

ABOUT *the* AUTHOR

Jeremy S. Adams is a social studies teacher at Bakersfield High School in Bakersfield, California, and a political science lecturer at California State University, Bakersfield.

He has received numerous teaching honors, including the 2014 California Teacher of the Year Award from the Daughters of the American Revolution and the 2012 Kern County Teacher of the Year Award. In 2013, he was a semifinalist for the California Department of Education's Teachers of the Year Program, and in 2014, he was a finalist for the prestigious Carlston Family Foundation National Teacher Award. The California State Assembly and California State Senate have both sponsored resolutions recognizing Jeremy's achievements in education. In 2018, he became the first classroom teacher ever to be inducted into the California State University, Bakersfield, Hall of Fame.

Jeremy is the founder of the Earl Warren Cup, a constitutional competition that quizzes students' knowledge of U.S. civics and history. For the competition, he has obtained recorded questions from an assortment of influential people, including U.S. presidents, Supreme Court justices, congressional leaders, Hollywood and media celebrities, and foreign heads of state.

He has authored two books on teaching: *The Secrets of Timeless Teachers* (2016) and *Full Classrooms, Empty Selves* (2012). He and his writings have appeared in numerous national media outlets, including the *Washington Post*, the *HuffPost*, the *Los Angeles Times*, the *Sacramento Bee*, C-SPAN, and the Educator's Room. He frequently speaks to groups of teachers and other educators, whom he passionately motivates to adopt strategies and attitudes that help them find meaning and purpose in their profession.

Jeremy received his bachelor's degree in politics from Washington and Lee University and his master's degree in education (curriculum and instruction) from California State

University, Bakersfield, where he was named the Outstanding Student in the School of Education.

To learn more about Jeremy's work, follow @JeremyAdams6 on Twitter.

To book Jeremy S. Adams for professional development, contact pd@SolutionTree.com.

INTRODUCTION

Resilience accommodates the unexpected.
—JOHN LEWIS GADDIS

At the high school where I have spent my entire career, there was a brief period during which the students would not stop pulling the fire alarms. Every few days, multiple buildings on campus would have to evacuate for ten minutes or so. As one can imagine, this was disruptive and tiresome for everyone involved. Teachers got behind on their schedules, students were interrupted during tests, and the administration grew frustrated with clearing buildings that were not on fire. Eventually, the school installed security cameras in the hallways, and the problem quickly went away. But when the pulled alarms were still a problem, the students would invariably ask me, "Mr. Adams, if our building was really going up in flames and you could take only one object or possession, what would it be?"

I thought hard. There were many candidates. I desperately love my books. My diplomas would be difficult to replace. I would certainly miss the bust of Socrates that I bought in Athens if it was lost to a fire. But nothing approaches the importance of one particular file in my classroom cabinet that gets larger as the years go on. It contains all the letters written to me by current and former students. I suspect most teachers keep similar files in their classrooms.

My students are my life's work—my magnum opus. Since the task of a teacher is not creation but guidance and inspiration, these letters are the closest thing I will ever have to a painting, a symphony, or a sculpture. Whenever I'm having a bad day or going through a rough patch in my career, I open the file and read a letter written to me long ago. These letters and the sentiments they express remind me why I teach young minds.

These letters often act as flotation devices for my teacher morale, and I suspect they also serve this purpose for other teachers who hold on to these writings. We reach for these letters because teachers' jobs are getting harder as we move through the 21st century. The endless cycle of change in education places considerable stress on classroom teachers' everyday lives. The sources of change are numerous and diverse in content, and the changes seem to come in all forms and from all directions. They are often curricular, cultural, administrative, parental, and technological—just to name a few!

These changes affect every facet of our profession: the way we teach our classes, the way we communicate with parents and the broader public, the way we approach professional development and interact with colleagues and administrators, and so on. Unlike those who have professions that carry great stability and continuity of policy and expectation, teachers work in a professional space of perpetual disorientation. About the only constant is change itself—which is why this book will foster teachers' resilience and morale in the face of this change.

In the book, we'll explore how teachers can recognize and adapt to the changes that characterize the world of education, strengthen the relationships they've built within it, and actually thrive in their roles. Later in the introduction, I'll also explain how the book's unique structure can help readers home in on the concerns that are most relevant to them. This way, readers can—in a manner that suits how they learn and where they are in their careers—ensure that the classroom remains the chief place for transformative learning experiences and that they find hope and purpose at the center of it all.

Recognizing the Changes in Education

Unlike my school's fire-alarm problem, which had a simple, direct solution, meeting our constantly changing job requirements as 21st century educators is more complicated and involved, and it will require us to first understand and acknowledge how circumstances for teachers have changed. Indeed, the seed of this text began with an article I wrote for the educational website the Educator's Room; I titled it "10 Things Teachers DID NOT Have to Deal With 10 Years Ago" (Adams, 2018). As a writer, I dreamed of publishing content that goes viral, and I got my wish. The article *exploded*. Within a month, it had been viewed 114,000 times and shared almost 25,000 times. It was picked up and republished by the *Washington Post*'s popular education page *Answer Sheet* (Strauss, 2018). Clearly, the claim that the hurdles of educational success are getting higher struck a nerve in the corps of teachers.

Teachers who are in the middle of their careers know that the job is constantly changing and getting more difficult. Some perennial problems (poverty, lack of parental support, and threats to school safety) are getting worse, while some problems (pervasive student anxiety, strains associated with high-stakes testing, and the distraction of students' ubiquitous cell-phone usage) have arisen with 21st century developments.

Teachers are not imagining higher hurdles. A spate of ominous-sounding books like *The Teacher Exodus: Reversing the Trend and Keeping Teachers in the Classrooms* (Zarra, 2018) and *Demoralized: Why Teachers Leave the Profession They Love and How They Can Stay* (Santoro, 2018) continue to emerge. Simultaneously, teachers' websites gain traffic through posting provocatively titled pieces such as "The Exhaustion of the American Teacher" (Kuhn, 2013), "Why a Teacher Cannot Have a Normal Life . . ." (Trosclair, 2015), "Teacher Burnout or Demoralization? What's the Difference and Why It Matters" (Walker, 2018), and "Why Teachers Are Walking Out" (Nichols, 2018). What is most disconcerting about these articles is that they are autobiographical in nature. These are not dry journalistic tomes of discouraging data harnessed to justify minor policy changes or pedagogic tweaks. Instead, the teachers writing these articles are trying to sound an alarm bell, or at least elicit some community concern, about the profound changes occurring within the teaching profession in just a short amount of time. Their pleas are deeply personal. Their wisdom is born out of struggle, not detachment. Together these writings speak to an underlying reality that teacher stress and strain cannot be a figment of teachers' collective imaginations.

And yet many teachers enter the profession with positivity, optimism, and even idealism. Teachers at all grade levels and in all subject areas understand the classroom has a pulse of magical possibility in it; as teachers, we are imbued with the privilege of possibly making the ultimate difference in students' lives. The words travel writer Horatio Clare (2017) uses to describe a new journey in his book *Icebreaker: A Voyage Far North* could just as easily be the words and sentiments of teachers at the dawn of every school year: "I experience one of those leaps of the heart, of love and thrill for the world, a euphoric gratitude for life . . . for which there can be no one word in any tongue" (p. 2). A potent appreciation for a lifetime spent shaping and influencing young minds is why teachers in the twilight of their careers often possess a quiet but palpable sense of contentment. They are rarely rich or famous, yet they know that their careers have been forces for good in the lives of many people. They have experienced too many "leaps of the heart" to feel otherwise. So how do teachers negotiate 21st century stressors and the ambitious, passionate spirit that drove them into the profession in the first place?

Adapting to the Changes

A fellow history teacher in the district where I teach, who also happens to be my older and wiser brother, Howard, said something that I connected with as I was writing this book:

> The problem with the constancy of change for us teachers is that after a while it eventually just becomes noise. This is daunting on a million

different levels. But the worst part is teachers who can't cut through the noise never flourish. They just get by. (H. Adams, personal communication, December 2018)

Teachers at all grade levels, no matter where they find themselves in their careers, must be able to confront the constancy of change in education so that they do more than merely "get by." And my goal with this book is to assist them in doing so. I want to empower teachers *to flourish*. I want to impassion them to excel. The best teachers possess dexterous skills—some pedagogical and professional, some personal and intellectual—that allow them to successfully manage those changes that define the teaching profession. Thus, this book aims to help teachers adapt to the never-ending process of reform and change so that teaching remains both vital and meaningful to them.

As any veteran teacher can attest, there comes a moment in every teacher's life when the newest wave of reform no longer appears as an opportunity to ride higher and cultivate fresh skill sets. Instead, new waves become menacing in their constancy, forces of nature that must be endured if one is to continue the odyssey of classroom instruction. From this perspective, it should surprise no one that anxiety and apprehension are fixtures in the lives of teachers.

This book offers a sensible approach to change that is both sympathetic to the various difficult situations teachers often find themselves in and positive in the belief that teachers can find, or recover, the deeper meaning of everyday classroom instruction. Hence the title—finding this deeper meaning hinges upon teachers riding each wave of reform, recognizing it as one they can deftly navigate, not one that will surely overcome them. As David B. Cohen (2017), author of *Capturing the Spark: Inspired Teaching, Thriving Schools* (Cohen, 2016), has argued, "The question is whether or not educators can make choices or select strategies that seize the exciting potential of change without feeling so overwhelmed that we want to leave the field" (p. 34).

Strengthening Key Relationships

An oversimplistic view of teaching focuses exclusively on instruction between the teacher and student, and usually only on instruction that occurs within a traditional classroom setting for a prescribed amount of time per day. But teaching requires more than basic interaction with students—our commitment to education includes obligations, interactions, and relationships with colleagues, administrators, and the public. Thus, to equate education with teaching is to misunderstand both.

Teachers who enjoy their profession and prosper in it do so because of the relationships they cultivate: relationships with the students they teach, the colleagues they teach alongside, the administrators they report to, and the broader communities they serve. But during a time when schools' and teachers' professional responsibilities never seem to lessen, it is common, and natural, that we feel strained in ourselves and in our relationships. As any teacher can explain, these stresses and strains start at the individual level. And we carry them with us wherever we go. They haunt us even when we are not on the job or in the classroom.

To appreciate the magnitude of the strain that constant change places on teachers, consider the five concentric circles in figure I.1. Imagine that in the innermost circle is a mirror in which a teacher can view only the stress and strain within him- or herself. Every time the teacher steps back into a wider circle, a complex web of entangled relationships is revealed. When the teacher steps back from the first circle, it is obvious that the strain and stress of constant change also affect his or her relationships with students and the classroom. Another step back, and the teacher can see other teachers on campus and the ever-shifting dynamics among colleagues. The next step back reveals the office, filled with administrators attempting to implement macro policy on a micro level—a process rife with tension and anxiety for everyone involved. Finally, on the outermost circle, the teacher sees the community, which grows increasingly frustrated with schools and educational outcomes, while the teachers within these schools feel misunderstood and unappreciated by the public they serve.

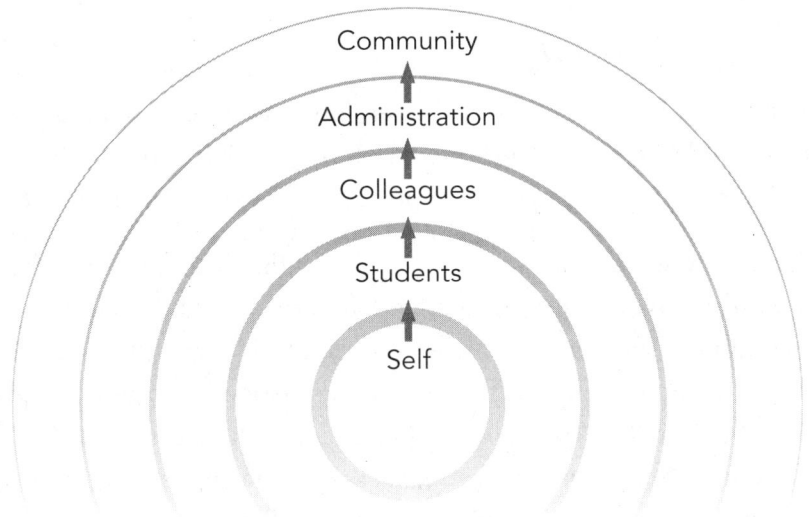

FIGURE I.1: Five relational circles of classroom teachers.

Each part of this text will address one of the five pivotal teacher relationships and common questions related to it.

- **Part 1: The Self**—How do constant changes in education affect a teacher's sense of self and individual well-being? What practices and strategies can teachers use to overcome the difficulties they face?
- **Part 2: Students**—What changes in policy, culture, and technology are making classroom life more difficult? How can teachers maintain strong relationships with their students amid these changes?
- **Part 3: Colleagues**—How does an environment in a state of flux alter the dynamics among colleagues on a teaching staff? What procedures and practices can ensure strong collaboration and a meaningful esprit de corps?
- **Part 4: Administration**—Why do adversarial relationships sometimes develop between administrators and their staff in an era of disruption and change? What can both parties do to avoid acrimony in favor of camaraderie and staff solidarity?
- **Part 5: The Community**—Why is there such a marked divergence between how the public views the quality of educational outcomes and how teachers view these outcomes? What can be done to bridge the gap?

This text attempts to repair each of these circles a teacher occupies, and it does so by focusing on pragmatic, research-based methods of sustaining the relationships teachers rely on to supply meaning and purpose in their careers.

Flourishing as an Educator

No one in education is immune to the tension caused by constant change—not teachers, not students, not administrators. Thus, the advice and lessons this book offers for flourishing amid change should prove helpful to an assortment of educators.

- **Experienced teachers:** Veteran teachers feel the weight of change because they have traveled a long road. They have experienced the relentless twists and turns of the education highway. Most of all, they are familiar with the frustration that comes from mastering a task or an expectation and then being told it is time to abandon what they have gotten used to. This frustration bears profound emotional and relational costs and is a primary concern that needs to be addressed in the profession. Denying this feature promotes burnout and a host of negative responses to one's career. This book, then, invites these veteran teachers to give their own well-being the attention it deserves—to recharge and recalibrate.

- **New teachers:** While veteran teachers can speak to the actual experience of enduring constant change, new and aspiring teachers must equip themselves with the strategies and tools that will be necessary to manage change throughout their careers. Most exemplars of the teaching profession hold it as an article of faith that teachers can always improve and there is always a fresh way to embody notions of classroom excellence. Doing what is required is a qualitatively different skill than knowing how to adapt and flourish when circumstances and expectations change. New teachers who come prepared to embrace the constancy of change will better position themselves to remain positive and purposeful in their careers. What the profession will require in five, ten, or thirty years is impossible to predict. We cannot know what turns lie ahead, but this book will help new teachers learn how to navigate them when they come—which they surely will.

- **Administrators:** Within the educational ecosystem, administrators exist in a professional space that can be exceedingly uncomfortable. On the one hand, they have almost no power in deciding which trends, expectations, or policies to implement—that power typically belongs to policymakers, district trustees, and superintendents. On the other hand, they have the arduous responsibility of making sure teachers on staff implement the reforms that are being required of them. They facilitate the training, oversight, and activities that serve to bring about the desired changes. Administrators feel the weight of reform in their relationships with staff and anyone actively involved in administering and enforcing reform. Because much of teachers' frustration occurs when administrators make their expectations unclear or communicate them in a manner that harms morale, this book will assist in creating positive lines of communication between administrators and their staff. Administrators will also familiarize themselves with the strain that constant change exerts on teachers and their classes. This will not only make administrators more empathetic but also equip them with tools to assist their teachers as they tackle changes together.

- **Teacher leaders:** In this context, *teacher leaders* refers to teachers playing leadership roles in districts or at school sites—the ones who decide which issues teachers need to address and how they should address them. One can't be an effective leader in a school or district without possessing an acute awareness of the different pressures teachers endure. With this book, leaders who help set policy or assist teachers in their practices will come to understand the causes of teacher difficulties and cultivate practices to successfully confront them. Teacher leaders have the power to facilitate the strategies suggested here, and they can bring them to their teachers and disseminate them to their staff and district. This text will be ideal for teacher book groups that meet to intensively explore new strategies and trends in the education profession.

This book's advice on how to maintain a positive outlook about working in education is both timely and timeless. It's timely because the research clearly shows that teachers feel overwhelmed by the broadening set of expectations being placed on their shoulders. And it's timeless because policymakers or the wider public cannot quickly reverse a trend so characteristic of 21st century teaching.

According to journalist Dylan Matthews (2018), policymakers, think-tank researchers, and billionaires have the habit of viewing classrooms as laboratories for social and economic innovation. In brief, many of these well-intentioned educational advocates and entrepreneurs have their hearts in the right place. But their focus is squarely on the *outputs* of the education system. Everyday teachers, on the other hand, must confront the harsh reality that social, economic, and familial *inputs* have monumentally changed the way we go about educating students. Outsiders to the teaching profession want schools to transform society, but the reality is that society has transformed schools.

Approaching the Book's Structure

This book is designed to be actionable and convenient. Its structure centers on the five concentric circles of pivotal teacher relationships (see figure I.1, page 5), with each part of the book focusing on one key relationship. The content throughout is intended to inform—and drive the behavior of—educators of all kinds, but the language and prompts are naturally geared toward classroom teachers, who are involved in *all* the relationships represented by the concentric circles. Many teachers will find all five parts relatable; however, some parts or chapters might not apply to every teacher. Therefore, readers may use each part independently from the others. For example, if teachers want to learn about self-care, they can refer to part 1 and don't necessarily need to read about combating the tensions that erupt between teachers and administrators in part 4. On that note, because administrators are key players in the relationships that part 4 covers in depth, this part is unique in that some recommendations are written with them in mind and directed at them specifically—so administrators will *not* want to skip it.

Each of the five parts is divided into two chapters. The first chapter in each part will answer the question, Why is there tension in this relationship? I will describe the nature of the problem teachers are encountering, demonstrate the problem's impact on teacher relationships, and explain why it is important to address. Each of these chapters includes multiple Notice the Wave prompts that invite the reader to pause for a moment and consider a particular issue in light of the information that I've presented.

While the first chapter of each part might seem overwhelming, with its enumeration and discussion of challenges, negative statistics, and various hurdles, readers should continue on, as the second chapter of each part will uplift, inspire, and comfort. That is, the second chapter is devoted to finding practical solutions to the problems that I've outlined; it offers detailed, research-based suggestions that can improve classroom teachers' chances of thriving amid change and finding or rediscovering meaning and purpose in their careers. This is where the book will lay out actionable guidelines for teachers, and each strategy will feature a Ride the Wave prompt that asks readers to tangibly articulate and record their thoughts and plans for the next steps through checklists, tables, graphic organizers, and written responses.

Note that strategies and Ride the Wave action pieces are designed to be intensely practical to those who are actively using this text to help address the problems associated with constant change. However, while each strategy or Ride the Wave is intended to facilitate practical assistance, it is not necessary for readers to engage each prompt in order to maximize the utility of the overall text. Teachers are free as classroom practitioners to pinpoint which problems, strategies, and action pieces are relevant to their specific troubles. In other words, each piece serves a purpose independently of the others. While I believe in the efficacy of the designed activities, they are not collectively more useful than when done on a one-by-one basis.

Finally, each chapter in the book will have a brief summary section that, for each *why* chapter, sums up the challenges or, for each *how* chapter, reminds us just what we can achieve now that we're armed with this knowledge and versed in the personal and collaborative fixes.

Recapturing the Magic

This book is a labor of love written by a teacher in the middle of his career. Twenty years in the classroom affords a unique perspective as it situates a teacher in a position as neither a novice nor a veteran on the cusp of retirement. On one hand, the beginning of my teaching career feels like forever ago. When I walked into my very first class, Bill Clinton was president, the 9/11 attacks were still three years from occurring, and Facebook and the iPhone did not exist. On the other hand, retirement and the wonders of a life free from the school calendar's constraints still feel so far out of reach that there is little use in trying to imagine them.

The good news is the mature perspective that comes from having taught for two decades means I have enough wonderful classroom memories to know that high-sounding phenomena—*splendor, enchantment, enthrallment*—are not just the province of movies and musicals. You don't have to visit Hollywood or Broadway to know these phenomena are real. They can, and should, make an appearance in the classroom. Sometimes, in the turbulence of change and disruption, the magic seems to vanish. This book is an attempt—albeit a modest one—to help teachers find this magic and to put it back where it belongs: in the classroom.

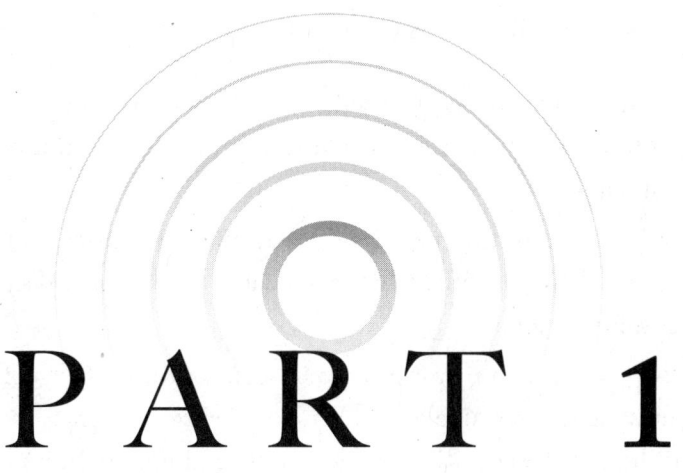

PART 1

the self

It's never overreacting to ask for what you want and need.
—AMY POEHLER

It's the stuff of an overwrought Hollywood screenplay.

A young man on the cusp of graduating from college has no idea what he wants to do with his life. On Thanksgiving break of his senior year, his elder sister unexpectedly passes away of congestive heart failure. He returns to school to take his final exams emotionally broken, empty, and at a loss. As he walks home by himself from class one afternoon, it hits him as hard as any idea has ever hit him in his entire life. He stops walking. He looks up at the broken clouds that have small sunrays poking through them. Suddenly, time folds in on itself, and he knows—truly, soulfully *knows*—what he wants to do with his life.

I used to tell this story—my story—to my students to let them know that I consider my job to be a calling, not a simple profession. "You know what happiness is?" I used to ask them. "It's knowing you are exactly where you are supposed to be in this life. It's the absence of daydreaming about being somewhere else and about doing something else."

I stopped telling this story to my teenage students. I figured either they would think I was being dramatic or they wouldn't know how it applied to them. Over the years, though, I have noticed that most teachers have their own tales to tell about their unique paths to the teaching profession. Their stories show that most teachers consider their craft to be an elemental part of their being. Teaching anchors them. It largely defines them. You can take them out of the classroom, but you can't take the classroom out of them. Even when they retire, they permanently bear the *teacher* label. However, when teachers experience constant change in education, it can place strain on their sense of self.

This reality raises a significant, perhaps even decisive, question about the teaching profession: How do challenges affect the teacher label and teachers' deep-seated, long-held belief that this is a calling?

It is imperative that we identify the origin and scope of the challenges facing teachers in the 21st century and determine how we, as conscientious professionals, can proactively confront these challenges. This process is valid and important no matter where a teacher finds him- or herself in a teaching career. It can help the new teacher in creating a professional identity; the established teacher in remaining relevant and effective in the classroom; and the nearing-retirement teacher in finishing on a positive note and extending his or her legacy. But we can achieve these ideals only if we are permitted—by ourselves and by others—to ride the wave of change by practicing self-care and giving proper attention to our well-being. When we understand the issues affecting teachers and develop healthy habits to neutralize them, it will ground us, sustain us, and allow us to confidently step into the classroom better prepared to serve students.

Ultimately, it is painful when teachers disengage from a profession they once celebrated. In the following pages, we'll understand why this schism emerges and, more to the point, what to do about it. It is natural as a teaching career progresses to experience decay or even boredom. But what an environment of unrelenting change unleashes is something closer to burnout and despair, propagating a feeling of alienation from one's own unique motivations for having entered the profession. To prevent such an outcome, a teacher must both notice the wave and learn how to ride it.

CHAPTER 1

Recognizing the Need for Self-Care

The last day of a teacher's career is instructive for those still teaching. Some teachers enthusiastically reach for the door of retirement without a single moment of pause or reflection. Most soon-to-be retirees, however, take the opportunity to look back at those of us still living the life of a classroom teacher. What they say to us is both fascinating and enlightening because teachers who stand at the door of retirement are usually imbued with a powerful tone of honesty. Sometimes their honesty is brutal, sometimes it is humorous, and sometimes it is inspiring. What they reveal is instructive because it is a form of pedagogic wisdom they wish they had received when they were younger, when they sat where teachers in the middle of their careers now find themselves. Honesty, it seems, can be hard to come by until the twilight of one's career.

Some remark on how much things have changed in schools and in society. Some reminisce about students and colleagues from long ago. Some tell amusing stories, while others simply break down in tears. But what they all express is a central truth about the teaching profession: the peaks of our profession are extraordinarily high, and the valleys are inordinately low. For typical teachers, the peaks and the valleys are almost always oriented around the lives of the students they teach, not the emotional states experienced by the teachers themselves. Notions of well-being and mental health are almost never discussed because such a discussion would place the teacher at the center of the educational universe. Many teachers, to their detriment, and until the end of their teaching days, are loath to think in these terms.

This job can and will make us weep, because sometimes, students disappoint or hurt us; colleagues frustrate or anger us; a nagging feeling tells us we are not the teachers we always dreamed we would be; and we feel powerless. Certainly, on my last day, far into the future, I will remember my dear friend and closest colleague, with whom I taught for almost two decades and who tragically died of cancer at the young age of forty. I will remember the agony of going into work the next day, of sitting in a classroom surrounded by the hundred students we had in common. I, like many teachers, will also remember decades of students who the world did not treat particularly well, who were victims of mental illness, substance abuse, or their own poor decisions. Indeed, a full account of a teaching career stares down into the valley of one's pain and disappointments, and the closing of my career will surely bring these feelings and experiences to the surface.

But upon retiring, I won't forget to look up at the many peaks that I traveled, recalling the classroom moments brimming with hope and transformation. I will almost certainly take pride in the contributions of my former students, some of whom are Broadway stars and some of whom are entrepreneurs and moguls within their professions. Hundreds are now teachers, and thousands do their part every day to make the world just a little bit better. Most of all, I will take delight in how many of them I now consider my friends.

Getting to the last day of one's teaching career—no matter if it is forty years or one year away—in a positive and impactful manner requires that one honestly assess just how difficult teaching can be for individuals within the profession. Teachers are often hesitant to reveal their struggles during their careers for fear of ever distracting from a student-centric learning environment, but this hesitation must end for a simple reason: an era of constant and unending change in education places unique pressures and burdens on teachers as individuals.

Learning how to conquer these challenges is no small task. But teachers can conquer them if they have the tools and wisdom necessary to address their struggles and maintain a positive, productive outlook during their career. Fortunately, we have wisdom in our midst—wisdom found in fellow teachers, voluminous educational research, and a shared and common profession. In this chapter, we'll make their wisdom our own by examining the cumulative toll of the 21st century, considering teacher stress and the symptoms of burnout, and identifying the positive effects of self-care.

The Cumulative Toll of the 21st Century

In *Take Time for You*, educational consultant and author Tina H. Boogren (2018) eloquently explains through a series of powerful inquiries why self-care ought to be at the forefront of educational concerns. She asks, "What if teachers learn to take care of themselves *while* taking care of their students? What if it weren't an either-or situation? What if you split your time between your own and students' needs in a new way?" (Boogren, 2018, p. 4). But why these questions? Why now? Why is self-care quickly becoming an increasingly talked-about subject in the realm of professional development?

Teachers in previous eras certainly encountered their share of high hurdles. As education historian Dana Goldstein (2014) observes in *The Teacher Wars*, at different times in American history "teachers have been embattled by politicians, philanthropists, intellectuals, business leaders, social scientists, activists on both the Right and Left, parents, and even one another" (p. 5). In the 1960s, national paranoia swept the land as Americans feared their Soviet counterparts would triumph over them in the disciplines of mathematics and science. The 1970s were embroiled in racial tensions stoked by concerns about integration and busing. The 1980s bemoaned a lack of cultural literacy. While many of these concerns have faded into the background of the nation's consciousness, the essential role the teacher plays in the maintenance of a growing and vibrant society firmly remains. This is why it is important to explore why there is something fundamentally different about the nature of teacher morale and strain in the 21st century.

As Patricia Jennings, a professor of education, notes (as cited in Garrison Institute, 2009):

> We ask an awful lot of teachers these days. . . . Beyond just conveying the course material, teachers are supposed to provide a nurturing learning environment, be responsive to students, parents, and colleagues, juggle the demands of standardized testing, coach students through conflicts with peers, be exemplars of emotion regulation, handle disruptive behavior and generally be great role models. . . . The problem is we rarely give teachers proper training or resources for any of them. (p. 1)

In April 2015, Steven C. Ward (2015) of *Newsweek* sought to answer the question, "Why has teacher morale plummeted?" In his article, he offers a variety of diverse and insightful explanations, ranging from teachers' "lost control of curricula" and the embrace of "edu-fashions" claiming to be one-size-fits-all solutions (for example, competency-based education, flipped classrooms, and the charter school movement) to "enrollment declining in teaching programs" (Ward, 2015). And as 2012 Connecticut Teacher of the Year David Bosso (2017) writes, "For a variety of reasons, but most certainly due to the increased demands of the evolving educational landscape, teachers often experience a discrepancy between the moral and affective purposes of their work and the external forces that affect it."

All these explanations have an element of truth to them. The constancy of policy changes is disorienting and frankly demoralizing—another common observation of new retirees. The frequency with which teachers are asked to absorb and master new trends (in technology, instruction, or social experimentation) is exhausting. In 2012, MetLife released a study titled *The MetLife Survey of the American Teacher*, and the study's executive summary and major findings sections both support the contention that teachers are battling the strains of endless reform yet are receiving a woeful lack of support (MetLife, 2012). Some disheartening highlights from this study's surveys, conducted in 2011, reveal the following (MetLife, 2012).

> Sixty-three percent of teachers reported that class sizes were increasing.
> According to 34 percent of teachers, "educational technology and learning materials [had] not been kept up to date" (p. 7).
> Almost two-thirds of teachers (64 percent) reported that the number of families requiring social support services had increased.

Clearly, classroom teachers are having to make do with insufficient materials while educating more and more students, many of whom are struggling outside school and may require extra care at school. Add all these factors together, and teaching in the 21st century has a psychological toll. The changing policy landscape coupled with the psychological stresses of education highlights the extent to which classroom instruction and teachers' perceptions of their place within the profession have categorically changed between 2010 and 2020 alone. The American Federation of Teachers (2017) reports that half of all teachers have experienced a significant decline in their enthusiasm for the job. Moreover, a significant portion of them (26 percent) do not even feel safe on the job, as they have been "bullied, harassed or threatened" (American Federation of Teachers, 2017, p. 4).

Teachers have long complained about the fact that they lack a voice in setting policy and they lack power in dictating the direction of education in their state or community; in fact, this shared feeling dates as far back as 1988, when the *New York Times* published an article titled "Study Shows Teachers Still Feel Left Out on Policy" (Daniels, 1988). Similarly, when teachers are in the midst of constant change, they feel a lack of power, as the challenges that confront them are often beyond their control. This feeling of powerlessness that accompanies mounting responsibilities and policy reform often results in so much stress that teachers don't realize they *can* control how they respond to challenges—or practice self-care. Indeed, it is no coincidence that the first chapter of this book tackles the issue of taking teacher self-care seriously.

> **NOTICE *the* WAVE**
> What are some examples of tasks and responsibilities you never thought you would have to take on when you first became a teacher? How did you initially respond to these tasks and responsibilities once they became your own?

Teacher Stress and the Manifestations of Burnout

Teachers face a daunting list of stressors. As professor Einar M. Skaalvik and scholar Sidsel Skaalvik (2007) note, "Stressors may include students with behavioral problems, problems in the parent–teacher relationship, conflict with colleagues, or having to organize teaching in new ways as a consequence of working in teams or because of school reforms" (p. 613). But this is just part of the picture. For many teachers, the weight and worry of the unknown is also a great source of stress. They ask themselves, "What will problematic students do *tomorrow*?" and "What new reform will I need to adjust to *next year*?"

This stress and uncertainty may disturb teachers' sense of their own capabilities. In their classic study on dimensions of teacher self-efficacy, Skaalvik and Skaalvik (2007) explain, "Self-efficacy beliefs are constructed largely on the basis of one's prior mastery experiences" (p. 621). In terms of a healthy perception of one's classroom efforts, self-efficacy occurs when teachers feel they are effective instructors and successful managers of desirable classroom outcomes. However, when stress and frequent changes enter the picture, teachers' levels of self-efficacy may decrease. Professors Robert Klassen and Ming Chiu (2010) find that high stress and low self-efficacy are strongly correlated, so teachers with great levels of stress tend to experience low levels of self-efficacy. Even the very best teachers can experience feelings of low self-efficacy if they are hit with enough stressors. Indeed, low self-efficacy is more a consequence of being overwhelmed in the classroom than it is a lack of pedagogic or subject-matter competence.

High levels of stress and low self-efficacy make for a dispirited corps of teachers. MetLife's (2012) study reveals that teachers experienced a 15 percent drop in job satisfaction in two years and the percentage of teachers who voiced the possibility of their leaving the profession increased by 12 percent in three years. American University's School of Education (2019) reports that many of the negative feelings associated with modern teaching—a lack of resources, low pay, negative political environments, too much emphasis on testing, and too much teaching to the test—are driving teachers from the classroom. On top of that are teachers' clear feelings of hopelessness, or futility, when it comes to the metrics by which many in and outside the profession define educational success, as only 43 percent of surveyed teachers believed student achievement would improve between 2011 and 2016 (MetLife, 2012). In the 21st century, capable teachers who may have entered their careers with confidence and positivity may end up feeling, frankly, burned out.

According to professor Ralf Schwarzer and scholar Suhair Hallum (2008), *burnout* is "a chronic state of exhaustion due to long-term interpersonal stress within human service professions. It pertains to feelings experienced by people whose jobs require repeated exposure to emotionally charged social situations" (p. 155). Indeed, most difficulties that teachers encounter in the profession are emotionally charged.

Schwarzer and Hallum (2008) quote the foundational work of Michael P. Leiter and Christina Maslach (1998) and argue that there are three symptoms of burnout: (1) emotional exhaustion, (2) depersonalization, and (3) reduced personal accomplishment.

1. **Emotional exhaustion:** When teachers say, "I am at the end of my rope," they mean they have emotional exhaustion. It is a juncture of one's career characterized by the sapping of one's emotional energy. Frequent symptoms of emotional exhaustion can include lethargy, fatigue, and even debilitation (Schwarzer & Hallum, 2008). This stress component is more than the physical exhaustion that results from being on one's feet for seven hours, engaging large numbers of students for whom the teacher has full responsibility. Instead, this manifestation of teacher burnout usually emerges after long exposure to stressful situations—situations that are often beyond the classroom teacher's control.

2. **Depersonalization:** When teachers pivot from a positive and enthusiastic professional disposition to a decidedly more cynical and negative one, they generally do so because the job itself has become depersonalized. Depersonalization occurs when a teacher, for whatever reason, no longer feels personally connected to the outcomes of the classroom in which he or she teaches. Teachers who speak of being "over it" or who claim to no longer feel invested in their teaching environment embody this component of burnout, which is more than a simple loss of idealism. Once a teacher depersonalizes his or her job, he or she will have difficulty reclaiming feelings of self-efficacy and success without undergoing intense reflection and professional assessment. This is why so many teachers either stop being personally invested in class outcomes or leave the profession altogether.

3. **Reduced personal accomplishment:** Schwarzer and Hallum (2008) equate reduced personal accomplishment with "reduced professional efficacy, productivity or capability, low morale, and an inability to cope with job demands" (p. 155). They also define it as feelings of intense inadequacy that often result in a teacher's lower assessment of his or her professional achievement (Schwarzer & Hallum, 2008). When a teacher dissociates classroom efforts with any expectation of achievement, then burnout has severely hampered any hopes of finding genuine joy and meaning in his or her educational endeavors. Teachers who claim to find no payoff for hard work, personal sacrifice, and intensive time commitments to their profession often withdraw from making any further commitments.

If teachers' stress levels are so high as to render them incapable of coping with job demands or recognizing the purpose of their role and commitment to education, their very well-being is compromised, thus making classroom instruction a painful slog from which they disengage (Schwarzer & Hallum, 2008). Journalist Kassondra Granata (2014) suggests this day-to-day learning environment is unsustainable for not only teachers but their students.

> ## NOTICE *the* WAVE
> Have you ever experienced any of the symptoms of teacher burnout—emotional exhaustion, depersonalization, or reduced personal accomplishment? What were the signs for you?

The Benefits of Self-Care

Teachers need to understand that self-care is not *indulgent*. In fact, it is the height of professionalism for a simple reason: when teachers are not at their best, our schools will not be at their best. When schools do not function in an optimal fashion, our students will not reach their full potential. Thus, responsible professional development must include a robust conversation about self-care. According to teacher and college instructor Jennifer Gonzalez (2017), far too many educators associate self-care with self-indulgence or professional weakness; they often feel guilty when they admit they need more information about self-care. Rather than seek this information, they maintain unproductive, strenuous work habits. As she writes in her popular blog *Cult of Pedagogy*, "Too many teachers have reached the conclusion that this [unhealthy] lifestyle is just part of the job; there simply isn't enough time to be a good teacher and take care of yourself" (Gonzalez, 2017).

Professor Keith Herman, doctoral student Jal'et Hickmon-Rosa, and professor Wendy Reinke (2018) note in a prominent study, "Teacher stress and burnout are significant problems that affect our schools. Finding innovative and impactful ways to improve outcomes for students by supporting teachers may make a significant contribution to society" (p. 98).

When teachers thrive emotionally, physically, and psychologically, the list of positive consequences is almost limitless. Consider that when students describe the qualities of effective teachers, they commonly observe that these teachers seem to enjoy what they are doing (Urban, 2008). The teachers want to be in the classroom. The classroom rejuvenates them. In short, the best teachers derive genuine joy and purpose from their interactions in the classroom (Adams, 2016). Self-care makes for more positive and productive classroom teachers—which makes for more positive and productive students.

Data confirm that when teachers feel good about themselves and their profession, they are more likely to provide a high-quality education to their students. Trauma consultant William Steele (2017), for example, has argued that teachers who eagerly practice self-care are far more likely to be proactive in reacting to both student challenges and overall challenges of the educational system. Self-care gives teachers the tools they need to effectively cope with the difficult circumstances of 21st century education.

> ## NOTICE *the* WAVE
> Do school staff talk about self-care at your school? If so, does it seem like a perfunctory conversation, or do both administrators and teachers take it seriously? If staff haven't brought up self-care, how do you think your colleagues would react to the topic?

Summary

Teaching has never been easy. Standing in front of dozens of young people for hours every single day can be challenging even in the most stable and supportive of environments. And sadly, most teachers feel that their jobs are more stressful in 2020 than they were in 2010. Everything is faster—the trends, the technology, the unpredictable disruptions to the profession itself—which adds to teachers' difficulty in maintaining a positive, productive frame of mind. Irrespective of the reasons for this shift in attitude and morale, it is no longer an option for schools to hope that teachers "get their minds right" or "find a happy place" on their own. In service professions such as teaching, there is sometimes a stigma associated with considering anyone besides those being serviced. But schools are communities, and while students are correctly the focal point, teachers should never hesitate to acknowledge their own limitations or needs as they relate to their roles within those communities. As long as we can count on constant change and reform, teacher self-care will remain a relevant and necessary topic in education. It must feature just as prominently in our professional conversations as pedagogy, credentialing, and technological trends do.

This chapter has explained why taking self-care seriously is important to maintaining the integrity of the teaching profession. In the next chapter, we'll learn a variety of self-care strategies teachers can use inside and outside of school. These strategies will help teachers maintain a sense of control over their health and career and prepare themselves each day for whatever the classroom has in store.

CHAPTER 2

Practicing Self-Care

Now that the case for self-care has been made, let us discover how to put theory into practice. The following five strategies will help you maintain your personality as an educator, avoid compassion fatigue, better manage your stress, self-reflect in a fairer way, and keep a positive outlook amid negative situations. Depending on your experiences and mindset, you may find some strategies more useful than others, but know that each strategy represents just one component of your well-being and effectiveness as a classroom teacher.

Strategy 1: Stay Yourself

At one point or another, almost every teacher has faced an intimidating reform—such as incorporating new technologies, flipping classrooms, confronting students' emotional issues, or conducting an unorthodox lesson—and thought to him- or herself, "You've got to be kidding. That isn't me! I can't do that."

When facing change, you must stay yourself. As you will see, this can mean a multiplicity of different things. But this much is certain: resistance to reform is natural. When teachers don't feel suited to new educational developments, they may feel as if they must lose their teaching style and their entire self in the process of reform. But they can maintain their personalities during such changes. The idea is that you should never try to be a teacher you aren't. Teachers who master the ability to absorb new demands while maintaining who they are as individual teachers will stay positive and continue to flourish through turbulent times.

How do they achieve this duality? By realizing that they still have considerable power over their own classrooms. As researcher Mark Feng Teng (2017) observes, "There is an interconnection between teachers' professional identities and their sense of agency"

(p. 119). In more practical terms, what does this look like? Teachers can maintain a sense of control by:

- Implementing changes at their own pace
- Approaching change as an opportunity to add new color to their teaching canvas instead of as a demand to burn what they have already painted
- Holding on to unique personality traits or quirks
- Preserving assignments and activities that they especially enjoy or value

Funny teachers should retain their sense of humor. Teachers who tell stories should absolutely keep telling stories. Teachers who like a strict schedule should continue scheduling.

Sound reforms will allow for the natural diversity that exists among teachers who stand in front of the classroom day after day, week after week, and sometimes decade after decade. After all, there is a vast difference between a dictate to "change what you do in the classroom" and a dictate to "change who you are in the classroom." Teaching is an activity rooted in a common humanity and delivered with teachers' force of personality, and shedding that personality is fraught with drawbacks, such as feeling like a fraud or phony in front of one's students. Your personal teaching style is a reservoir of joy in the teaching profession. So if this style serves you and your students well, you should continue to drink from this reservoir and remain loyal to this style while confronting change. Your prosperity in the classroom and your experience of teaching's greatest rewards depend on your sense of agency and individuality amid constant change.

Strategy 2: Remember the Basics and Avoid Compassion Fatigue

Self-care might sound instinctual, but that is not necessarily so—not when teachers are expected to absorb every new policy and institute every change at a rapid pace, sometimes without understanding the why or how of the process. After a while, this cycle takes its toll.

Working in the classroom for long periods of time can impair a teacher's ability to know the difference between what is essential to self-care and what is optional. Essential self-care encompasses behaviors that allow a teacher to maintain a healthy, positive disposition in the classroom and to remain optimistic about the profession itself. When teachers get some distance from their everyday tasks, they can see what is sometimes difficult to discern in the middle of a school year, surrounded by students and immersed in an overwhelming number of daily responsibilities. However, teachers have basic self-care opportunities that will promote a productive state of mind for the

RIDE *the* WAVE
STRATEGY 1

List four to five classroom routines or aspects of your personality that you would never change, no matter the reform being instituted. Below each, explain why it is so important to you and your sense of who you are.

1.

2.

3.

4.

5.

*Visit **go.SolutionTree.com/teacherefficacy** for a free reproducible version of this feature box.*

classroom. For example, teachers should take advantage of their no-tell days—official time off in which they do not have to provide the reason for their absence—or try to take short trips on weekends to decompress. Those who are spiritual should nurture that aspect of themselves. And teachers should feel free to enjoy activities for their own sake, rather than operating as though everything must have a broader goal.

If a teacher has a defective perspective on self-care or doesn't take advantage of these recharging activities, then he or she may experience *compassion fatigue*. This means his or her capacity to relate to and empathize with students has ebbed, despite the best of intentions. The National Child Traumatic Stress Network (NCTSN, 2008) rightly argues that the "best way to deal with compassion fatigue is early recognition" (p. 17) and offers self-care tips for educators that ensure they cover the basics. While NCTSN's (2008) list centers on teachers who instruct traumatized students, in reality, these suggestions are applicable to all teachers. They are broad but pragmatic enough to put into action.

> **Be aware of the signs:** Compassion fatigue is characterized by irritability, a lack of motivation to teach or plan lessons, decreased levels of concentration, and an inability to empathize with students or with traumatic events. Teachers teetering on the verge of such a state often complain that they simply don't feel like themselves or that they don't know how much more they have to give.

> **Don't go it alone:** Isolation is the enemy. Use the school's and administration's resources to find the support you need in whatever form is appropriate. Teachers who find themselves in stressful situations with students need to know they are not alone. In real terms, this might mean seeking advice from a mentor teacher, a former master teacher, or any experienced educator whose advice you especially value.

> **Recognize compassion fatigue as an occupational hazard:** It is not a sign of weakness for teachers to sometimes feel numb to the circumstances of their students. It is merely an outgrowth of the limits one has in processing, understanding, and empathizing with all students' circumstances. Compassion is not a finite resource for teachers. And while it can certainly be fleeting at times, especially in periods of great stress and strain, there is no reason why it cannot be recovered.

> **Talk to a professional:** If you show signs of significant stress or compassion fatigue for more than two or three weeks, then seeking the counsel of professionals is well advised. School districts are increasingly helpful in recommending professional help—as are insurance providers. Or you

may wish to visit Psychology Today (www.psychologytoday.com/intl), where you can search for therapists by insurance provider, location, gender, specialization, and so forth (Psychology Today, n.d.).

> **Attend to individualized self-care:** As NCTSN (2008) notes in its tips to educators:
>
> > Guard against your work becoming the only activity that defines who you are. . . . Take care of yourself by eating well and exercising, engaging in fun activities, taking a break during the workday, finding time to self-reflect, allowing yourself to cry, and finding things to laugh about. (p. 17)
>
> You are not a bad teacher if you insist on using your lunch break as an actual lunch break. You are not a failing educator if you want some time during recess or between passing periods to yourself. You are not selfish if you take the occasional no-tell day to sleep in, do laundry, or have fun.

Confronting constant change takes a toll that often goes unrecognized until teachers are already burned out and demoralized, so actively adopting these habits will go a long way in fostering self-care for teachers, no matter the population they teach.

Strategy 3: Learn the Difference Between Good and Bad Coping

Every teacher has a unique way of coping with stress, and teachers hoping to successfully confront challenges and changes will need to reflect on their go-to strategies. Professor Cameron Montgomery and research director André Rupp (2005) make a distinction between active coping and passive coping strategies, and they say the most effective teachers thoughtfully embrace the former.

Teachers frequently engage in passive coping, but this coping style is usually detrimental to the long-term viability of teaching success. Montgomery and Rupp (2005) pinpoint a number of passive coping behaviors, including "resignation, drinking, wishful thinking, and avoidance" (p. 468). These behaviors in turn can result in "anxiety, depression, or even suicidal ideation" (Montgomery & Rupp, 2005, p. 468). Passive coping strategies are almost all short term in nature and can be broadly described as avoidances of taxing classroom realities. Such strategies don't fix the root of the problem but rather delay a person's facing those problems he or she must inevitably deal with.

Active coping, on the other hand, generally takes the form of "cognitive strategies" such as "changing perspective," "exerting self-control," and "rationally distancing oneself" (Montgomery & Rupp, 2005, p. 468). This form of coping can also be emotional

RIDE *the* WAVE
STRATEGY 2

List up to five colleagues whose advice you value. These are people you would call on first if you needed advice or if you simply wanted to vent. Next to each name, write a sentence or two about why you think he or she would be a good person to seek out.

1.

2.

3.

4.

5.

in nature and involve "setting limits for work," "seeking advice from others," and "engaging in relaxation exercises" (Montgomery & Rupp, 2005, p. 468).

Active coping mechanisms provide you with cognitive and emotional capacities that will empower you, as a classroom teacher, to contextualize your teaching life by enhancing your perspective on your career and personal life. For example, a particular year of teaching may be trying, but an affirming form of coping will allow you to recognize that the difficult period will eventually end. A specific student may be challenging, but a successful episode of active coping will help you realize that most students are not difficult or a source of frustration. Also, active coping helps you realize that although your job might be a source of stress, that does not negate the blessings of your home life or remove all the interests you have outside of school.

Strategy 4: Be Self-Reflective and Set Realistic Goals

Change can distort what success and failure look like and make the very definitions of success and failure take on different qualities and appearances. As a result, constant change may create uncertainty over how teachers ought to feel about the outcomes they experience in their classrooms. Teachers can find it very difficult to self-reflect in the aftermath of a disappointing school year or in the face of new changes. However, four helpful reflective practices will allow teachers to process past outcomes in a relatively painless way yet aspire to turn failures into future successes. For all the suggestions that follow, it is important that teachers talk to one another about the lists and goals they create for themselves—otherwise, these are just mandatory exercises done in isolation. Because some of these suggestions require writing and all of them could reasonably involve the writing process, it might be wise for teachers to invest in a journal so that when they self-reflect and set goals, they have a single dedicated place to record and revisit their thoughts.

1. **Write down three disappointments and three successes from the school year a few weeks after the school year ends:** Give yourself a few weeks of perspective before making this list. The end of the year often leaves teachers feeling raw and run-down, even when the school year has been successful or concluded on a positive note. But with a bit of perspective, teachers can self-reflect in a manner that is not unduly negative or triumphant. Even the best years of a career can be improved on. Even the most dreadful years have their highlights. Making these lists will allow you to chart a realistic path to improvement that is both helpful for the future and comforting as you process the disappointments along the way.

RIDE *the* WAVE
STRATEGY 3

Researchers Vicky Austin, Surya Shah, and Steven Muncer (2005) offer the following list of activities for coping with teacher stress. Place a check mark next to each activity you have done and an *X* next to each one you wish to do in the future.

_____ Being active in a social club

_____ Being busy

_____ Being by myself

_____ Bicycling

_____ Breathing deeply

_____ Crying

_____ Eating

_____ Exercising

_____ Jogging

_____ Listening to music

_____ Preparing for work

_____ Relaxing or lying down

_____ Running long distances

_____ Screaming

_____ Sleeping

_____ Taking a hot bath or shower

_____ Talking to a friend

_____ Throwing something

_____ Visiting friends

_____ Walking

Source: Adapted from Austin, V., Shah, S., & Muncer, S. (2005). Teacher stress and coping strategies used to reduce stress. Occupational Therapy International, 12*(2), 63–80. Accessed at www.onlinelibrary.wiley.com/doi/pdf/10.1002/oti.16 on July 17, 2019.*

Visit go.SolutionTree.com/teacherefficacy for a free reproducible version of this feature box.

2. **Write about your best moment and worst moment from the school year:** Writing is a form of catharsis. It also triggers thought and reflection. Simply writing about an event—especially one that you have thought about over and over—can help you see the event in a different way. Writing it down in a straightforward manner can bring closure to a difficult moment and preserve moments that are worth remembering. This practice can provide a new, more nuanced layer of introspection, and sometimes, it brings clarity to the moment so that you better understand what made it so good or so bad. If nothing else, you will now better remember a moment that in the future might have eluded you.

3. **Reflect on why the disappointments happened, and create an action plan for next school year:** There are dozens of reasons why classes, units, or entire years sometimes fail to meet expectations. And there are different forms of disappointments. Was class rapport lacking? Was performance poor? Did you fail to get through all the curriculum, or did you mismanage your time? Was the school itself in crisis or suffering from a vacuum of leadership? Did your private life interfere with goals and outcomes? Objectively reflecting on the year's letdowns allows you to emerge from the negative headspace you may have been in, and to look back and see where you were situated the entire time. The next part is intensely personal. How are *you* going to be different next year? Were there factors within your control that you can handle better next year? Again, part of self-care is self-reflection—being honest with yourself about successes and failures and using that process to inform your future efforts. In the context of self-care, honestly assessing yourself and creating an action plan moving forward need not be excessively complicated.

4. **Pick four specific goals (one for each quarter) that you plan to implement next school year:** It can sometimes be easy to rest on your laurels in teaching. Doing the same thing year after year is a staple of the profession. But even if every lesson of every day is a teaching masterpiece, intentionally changing things up a little will help your teaching outlook. There is so much curriculum widely available, and so much technology that can enhance and complement classroom instruction, that it would not be too difficult to commit to doing something different or new at least once a quarter. It can be big or small, a tweak or a complete revision. It might sound odd to suggest that teachers can achieve self-care by doing more work, especially during summer break, and this certainly qualifies as work. But if the aim of

self-care is to help teachers feel better about their profession going forward, then goal setting can be a useful and fun enterprise; trying new things can supply elements of anticipation and excitement that a classroom might otherwise lack. Take the time to try something new—even if it means a little more effort. If you're an English teacher, introduce to your students a book you've never taught before. If you're a history teacher, create a new activity or assignment around a topic you've taught in the past. Whatever you do, you won't regret it when the new year begins.

Strategy 5: Optimize Optimism

The teaching profession is ripe with reasons why a classroom might not succeed. If teachers want to find a culprit for their professional failures, there are certainly many to be had: parents, policymakers, culture, funding, low pay, high and unending expectations—the list could go on and on. As a teaching career progresses, every teacher knows the temptation to shrug indifferently or react cynically to new challenges and methods. The classroom can be a tough place to stay hopeful and positive, but staying optimistic is crucial to teacher self-care's central purpose, which is to ensure that the teacher can teach at an optimal level in the face of constant change.

The following five strategies will help frustrated teachers gain a more nuanced and joyful perspective on their jobs. Even if they don't propel teachers to a summit of professional bliss, these powerful exercises can minimize the disappointments along the way. Teachers can use them to foster a positive perspective at any time and in any manner—at the end of a school year, during the summer, or even after an especially taxing day. These prompts can serve as mental exercises, or you may wish to write down your responses.

1. **Focus on what worked, not what didn't:** Or, to phrase it another way, focus on the students who behaved; who performed well; and who were courteous, kind, and hardworking. Teachers who feel the strain of change can develop the habit of mentally focusing on only the few who cause problems as they teach a classroom full of students. Most teachers do not need to work very hard to identify disappointments, but more than likely, successes are present as well. It just requires a little more diligence and digging to discover them.

2. **Put one class or year into its proper career context:** To stay positive, think of one school year as a single slice of your entire career. Do not conclude, "I no longer enjoy my profession," "The students don't listen anymore," or

RIDE *the* WAVE
STRATEGY 4

Are you somebody who likes to offer counsel to others? Do you find it rewarding to help other teachers on staff with their problems? List five ways in which you could be of assistance to others on your campus. Because teachers are often their own worst critics, it is useful to pinpoint what encouraging, affirming assessments you can offer up to those with whom you work.

1.

2.

3.

4.

5.

*Visit **go.SolutionTree.com/teacherefficacy** for a free reproducible version of this feature box.*

any other discouraging thought that runs through a vexed teacher's mind. Refrain from making definitive generalizations about your tenure based on isolated circumstances. A taxing year does not negate or lessen the positive outcomes that occurred in prior years of teaching. After all, talented composers sometimes choose the wrong note. Well-regarded authors sometimes don't write their best prose. Moreover, do not assume that once a career veers into a negative direction, it will necessarily stay that way. One year might be difficult, but that doesn't mean the next one will be as trying. Athletes often follow a bad game with a good game. A film director can follow a box-office bomb with a blockbuster. Teachers should believe that they can do the same.

3. **Remember that you can control only what's in front of you:** Almost all people in education—teachers, administrators, and support staff—have heard this advice before, and often, it doesn't make them feel any better. But it should. So many things go into the success and failure of education beyond what happens in a classroom—from parenting and culture to funding mechanisms and cyclical poverty. Staying optimistic will be easier if you remember you can control only what is in front of you. Extraordinary teachers can occasionally make huge leaps and overcome structural barriers and other high hurdles. But at the end of the day, you will do well to remember that incremental improvement is a victory. You cannot change the world your students come from, but you can use your time in the classroom to modestly improve your students' chances of eventual success.

4. **Remember your favorite teachers:** How many of your favorite teachers were naysayers? Probably not many. Whenever you find yourself sliding into the alluring grip of pessimism and despair, try to remember your favorite teachers. The best classes are almost always taught by teachers who make it clear they enjoy the subject, the students, and the lessons they teach. The most effective teachers are almost always optimistic, because they believe what students learn in a classroom can echo beyond the corridors of the school. Even if an optimistic demeanor feels forced or false, it is better than allowing cynicism to reign supreme. As superintendent Stephen R. Donovan (2014) notes:

> I have noticed in my school district that some of the most effective teachers appear to be those teachers who seem to remain confident in their ability to make a difference with all students,

despite the numerous obstacles that can impact the learning process. (p. 8)

5. **Remember that most classroom successes go unacknowledged:** Why do you know that the capital of Texas is Austin? Why do you know that the ancient Greek Euclid is the father of geometry? How do you know how to spot a double dribble in basketball? In life, we acquire knowledge, skills, and various capacities along the way, often without noticing it. But just because a person does not know that you helped him or her read, write, or critically think does not mean you have not been a success. In fact, most classroom successes go unacknowledged. Sometimes students are too young to appreciate their teachers. Sometimes people don't remember who is responsible for their skill sets and education. Try to remain optimistic by understanding that the classroom successes exist; it's just that the failures of the classroom are usually highlighted and the successes are often taken for granted. The totality of what teachers achieve in the classroom is impossible to measure, yet it is substantial. Acknowledge and remember your classroom successes along the way. As a fellow teacher once said to me, "Teachers need to learn the art of being a great chef—taste their own cooking and congratulate themselves regardless of what the consumer thinks."

Summary

This chapter has offered simple strategies for starting the process of self-care. Just as every teacher has unique strengths and weaknesses and a distinctive classroom personality, so, too, will different teachers require different levels and forms of self-care. Some teachers may simply need the occasional chance to vent to a friend, while others may require intensive professional guidance. But the need for self-care is universal. Every teacher, whatever his or her level of experience or difficulty, needs to find ways to cope with the stresses of the 21st century classroom so that our students have the best-possible chance to learn in positive, effective learning environments. To this end, teachers who wish to successfully confront constant change must take self-care as seriously as anything else in the profession.

RIDE *the* WAVE
STRATEGY 5

List three to four specific qualities of your favorite teachers. In what ways did these teachers from your past use these qualities to exhibit or bolster optimism in their classrooms? Next, reflect on the kindest words *you* have ever received from students about your teaching style. In what ways are the students' comments indicative of classroom optimism?

1.

2.

3.

4.

*Visit **go.SolutionTree.com/teacherefficacy** for a free reproducible version of this feature box.*

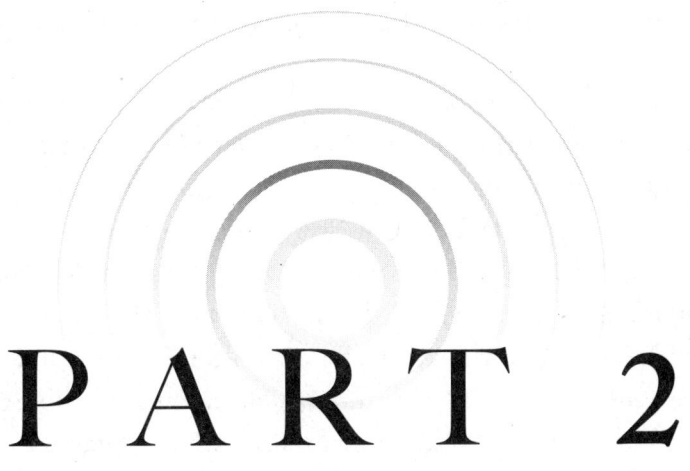

PART 2

students

*Better than a thousand days of diligent study is
one day with a great teacher.*
—JAPANESE PROVERB

Senior night is a big deal at the high school where I teach. It occurs in the late fall, when the weather has finally cooled and seniors are fully engrossed in the unique tasks of applying to college or securing plans for postgraduation.

The main event takes place immediately before the Friday-night varsity football game, and it is a dramatic scene. Senior football players, band members, and cheerleaders start walking from one end zone while the students' parents or guardians start walking from the opposite end zone. They meet at the fifty-yard line, and the students give their parents or guardians roses. Senior night usually occurs right before Thanksgiving, which is appropriate and symbolic; by this point in the year, seniors have started to realize how fast the end of high school is approaching, and they feel anxious—but thankful that their parents have been there for them, shepherding them with every form of support that they need.

One year, the student who wore the school mascot's costume approached me a few days before the senior night event. I knew he came from a difficult background, but I never imagined just how difficult it was. His father had been in prison for many years, and his mother was ill. He asked me whether I would meet him at the fifty-yard line and stand in for his parents. He was a delightful student, and I was of course happy to oblige.

It wasn't until a few months after his request that I came to a deeply upsetting realization: educators and schools fulfill much different roles in the 21st century than they did when I became a schoolteacher in the late nineties. In the infancy of my career, teachers generally thought of themselves in strictly pedagogical terms. Teachers could be role models. They could be mentors. They could at times be parental in their function. But never in my wildest dreams could I have imagined that I might be standing in for students' parents—doing, for example, what their fathers would have done in earlier generations. In 21st century schools, we stand up for students when other institutions stand down. We advocate for them when other influences are silent. We meet a growing need to address their stress and anxiety. We are their last line of defense between hope and hopelessness. The pressures these expectations place on our profession make our jobs hard but also transformative.

The waves of change adversely affect teachers. They adversely affect students. But let us not forget a third consequence—these enhanced expectations for teachers create unique tensions between teachers and their students. As teachers are asked to do more, the nature of young people is to resist external control or to ask more of teachers than teachers are accustomed to providing. Tensions mount when students don't receive enough personalized attention. Tensions mount when teachers institute restrictions on device usage that students may view as arbitrary and draconian.

When most people imagine a teaching career, they solely visualize an adult providing instruction, surrounded by students; this is just one small piece of the craft in the 21st century. Most teachers could offer dozens of anecdotes about now-commonplace classroom experiences that they never expected to have when they began their teaching careers. It is essential that we, as teachers, explore both what causes changes to education and what we should do about them. Learning how to ride the wave of robust change and thrive in the classroom is the undeniable goal of all the professional development that we do. With this in mind, let us begin.

CHAPTER 3

Understanding Stress Among the Desks

My father began his teaching career in the fall of 1972. I have heard plenty of stories about those early years from his former students. Some of them are surely apocryphal, as they include tales of uncharacteristically flamboyant fashion choices—bell-bottoms and loud red jeans are frequently mentioned—but the stories also tell of a young teacher destined to be the enthusiastic, first-rate educator he became. He didn't let anybody hide, he bounced around the classroom, and he saw any educational competition available to him—speech tournaments, spelling bees, any event where a trophy might be awarded to a student following a spirited match—as a chance for excellence. I have often wondered what it would be like to travel back in time and observe my father in the infancy of his teaching career, before he met my mother, before I was even a twinkle in his eye.

If I arrived in 1972 and walked across the campus where he taught, I am sure I would be shocked at the number of sights and norms that have been outmoded in the 21st century—the smoking rooms for teachers; the class offerings, which included sewing and driver's education; the students who walked around with their hands free and their heads held high, blissfully unaware that their grandchildren would one day become addicted to devices yet to be invented.

But what would probably surprise me the most about this time would be the universal understanding among staff and administration that schools were primarily about education and that teachers were primarily there to teach. What happened before a student entered, and after a student left, the classroom was not really the teacher's concern. Teachers viewed their jobs strictly in terms of content and pedagogy. If students had mental-health issues, those were the domain of counselors or psychologists off campus. Testing was localized, and curriculum was written at a grassroots level. Schools held rallies for football games, not schoolwide testing.

Whenever I imagine going back to my father's first school, however, I quickly realize that this is not necessarily a time or place to romanticize—kids were bullied, certain groups were marginalized and made the objects of epithets and scorn, and student learning seems to have been exclusively teacher centered in most classes. Not to mention chalkboards were the zenith of educational technology.

But still, the teaching profession had stability. In 1972, today's expectations were the same as yesterday's, and those expectations probably wouldn't change tomorrow. When failure occurred, the impetus for change was on the student, and blame was pointed outside the classroom. Today, failure is almost exclusively placed on the shoulders of teachers and schools. As author Kevin K. Kumashiro argues (as cited in Long, 2012):

> When you then talk about the problems in education, all eyes turn to the teachers—they aren't working hard enough, or they're too greedy, or they're not accountable. . . . The debate becomes about fixing individuals teachers—how do we incentivize them, how do we get rid of the lazy ones, how do we weaken their union "bosses."

Deep down, I know that each era has its unique challenges, but I can't help but feel that most teachers I'd encounter in 1972 and the decades beyond—my father included—wouldn't recognize their profession if they came to the 21st century with me. They'd certainly be struck by our never-ending to-do list and the devices and social media platforms that interfere with instruction, and they'd be alarmed by teachers' roles as they relate to the declining state of student mental health, the tightening testing regimen, and the perpetual school violence, which this chapter describes.

A Never-Ending To-Do List

When a problem arises in society, either it manifests itself in schools, or society looks to the schools to solve it. In both cases, the classroom is porous to the toxicity of culture, the failings of family life, and the ambitions of social engineers who view classrooms as both laboratories of change and meccas of meaningful policy experimentation. The classroom bears the marks of an era that increasingly assumes classrooms are panaceas for fixing social pathologies and sheltering students who are debilitated by a lack of familial support. The consequence is a plate filled with more and more professional obligations—to the point that teachers now wear so many hats and serve so many disparate student needs that the nature of the profession is overwhelming and difficult to define in concrete terms.

Researcher Suraj Kumar (2017) eloquently observes, in a survey of teachers:

> Almost every teacher interviewed identified as a growing challenge the organization of learning and management of exceptionally differing groups of students and what they saw as a social/passionate help part for students encountering challenges, including troublesome home conditions. The teachers must be both educated in their content area and extremely skillful in an extensive variety of teaching ways to deal with the different learning needs of each student. (p. 817)

Such conditions represent a gamut so wide that virtually any social or familial responsibility could be placed within it. Teaching truly is "one vocation, numerous parts" (Kumar, 2017, p. 817). Consider how much tension, stress, and anxiety educators experience due to the long list of expectations present in classrooms—expectations that educators must concurrently meet. An educator doesn't check off the following items one by one by the end of the year; he or she must juggle them every day, with each student, in a continual loop of intensive conscientiousness.

- Engage in behavior modification, and serve as a role model.
- Teach curriculum in a way that is sometimes traditional, sometimes avant-garde, always student centered, and concurrently teacher facilitated.
- Inculcate study skills in a way that is both rigorous and forgiving.
- Encourage self-reliance without forgetting the value of teamwork.
- Prepare students for civic life in a democracy.
- Prepare students for a challenging and versatile global economy.
- Emotionally support students while maintaining a high wall of professionalism, respecting boundaries, and being on the lookout for emotional and physical abuse.
- Intellectually challenge students, but don't damage self-esteem in the process.
- Make sure no one gets left behind.
- Be culturally aware.
- Enforce schoolwide learning expectations while upholding general norms of pedagogical protocol.
- Stage interventions, even if they are before school, after school, or during lunch.

- Prepare students for tests, but don't "teach to the test."
- Cultivate empathy, practice sympathy, and never allow students to feel unsupported.
- Don't forget critical thinking, but be mindful of imagination.
- Be on the lookout for bullies, belligerent students, and underserved populations.
- Use technology, but remember it should never supplant good teaching.
- Communicate with parents, collaborate with colleagues, and keep up with professional development outside the classroom.
- Never make excuses for any kind of classroom failure.

This list of responsibilities raises many questions about the intensity and variety of tensions that may develop between teachers and their students: Do students feel that teachers, in their zest to achieve too many outcomes, lose sight of their primary academic responsibilities? Do students feel disappointed by classrooms that aren't meeting their unique needs and desires? Do teachers begin to resent that students' needs are growing as their own resources and time are in finite supply?

This list—which is far from exhaustive—and the associated tensions call to mind a powerful quote in the history of educational research from psychologist Lee Shulman (2004), who famously observed, "After some thirty years of doing such work, I have concluded that classroom teaching . . . is perhaps the most complex, most challenging, and most demanding, subtle, nuanced, and frightening activity that our species ever invented" (p. 504).

The preceding list doesn't even consider all our responsibilities outside the classroom, where we are expected to be advocates, serve on committees, and advise numerous activities on campus. Yet this doesn't prevent the world of education from assigning new responsibilities and expectations to teachers.

NOTICE *the* WAVE

This section presented a long list of responsibilities that 21st century teachers are expected to juggle. Are there any important items left off the list? How does such a long list contribute to the stress and strain that classroom teachers experience every day?

Proliferating Platforms and the Problems They Breed

In "I Used to Be a Human Being," an eloquent essay about the profound changes smartphones have evoked in everyday life, former editor of the *New Republic* Andrew Sullivan (2016) challenges the reader:

> Just look around you—at the people crouched over their phones as they walk the streets, or drive their cars, or walk their dogs, or play with their children. Observe yourself in line for coffee, or in a quick work break, or driving, or even just going to the bathroom. Visit an airport and see the sea of craned necks and dead eyes. We have gone from looking up and around to constantly looking down.
>
> If an alien had visited America just five years ago, then returned today, wouldn't this be its immediate observation? That this species has developed an extraordinary new habit—and, everywhere you look, lives constantly in its thrall?

This habit is also on prominent display in the classroom. Virtually every feature of students' lives has been transformed or affected by the omnipotence of smartphones and the proliferating platforms they usher in. Instagram, YouTube, Twitter, Snapchat, and other platforms that may fly under even the most vigilant parents' radar are the social arteries for young people who spend long hours engaged with media. These media have largely supplanted traditional modes of communication and socialization—talking on the phone, spending time together, attending school-sponsored social events, and so on. And, according to Leah Shafer (2018) of the Harvard Graduate School of Education, students use social media not only for relational interactions but also for self-expression, exploration, and browsing.

These changes in communication and knowledge exchange have been rapid and severe, and most alarming of all, they are unlikely to slow down. According to a digital report authored by Simon Kemp (2019), 45 percent of the world's population now uses social media, an expanding number that represents three and a half billion people. The average daily time spent on the internet and using social media via any device adds up to eight hours and thirty-five minutes. The pace of change is as dizzying for professional educators as it is mystifying for all adults who do not exist in the same online world as students, a world that often has its own norms, expressions, and expectations.

Though not all the findings are catastrophic, data show that smartphones and the digital world they create affect our students' behavior in and out of the classroom and thus pose significant challenges for teachers at all grade levels. For example, Jean M.

Twenge (2017a), a professor of psychology, finds that in the 1970s, the average student read three times as many books as the average student does today. Perhaps even more startling is that students are more likely to read books when they are thirteen than when they are seventeen, according to journalist David Denby (2016). As they move further into their teens, students seem to replace books with "scraps, excerpts, articles, parts of articles, messages, pieces of information from everywhere and from nowhere" (Denby, 2016).

Research specialist Amanda Lenhart's (2015) Pew Research Center study reports that 92 percent of U.S. teens are online every day, with 24 percent reporting that they are "using the internet 'almost constantly'" (p. 16). Matthew Johnson (2015) of the Vanier Institute of the Family reveals that as Canadian students age, they become increasingly autonomous in how they navigate the internet and different social media platforms. In grade 4, 64 percent of students are reliant on a family computer to access the internet. By grade 11, that number drops to 37 percent, largely because 85 percent of Canadian teens have their own devices by their junior year (Johnson, 2015). A U.S. teen typically receives and sends thirty texts a day—many of which are likely transmitted during school hours (Lenhart, 2015). Sadly, the students sitting in our classrooms experience a variety of stressors as a result of their engagement with smartphone technology, what Twenge (2017b) describes as "the deleterious effects of 'screen time.'" Shafer (2017) condenses the Pew study by pinpointing the following stressors tied to students' devices and their social lives.

> - Observing posts about events they were not invited to (though 21st century students go to fewer parties and spend far less time together in the same physical place than previous generations of students)
> - Experiencing pressure to post attractive content or positive interactions
> - Feeling the need to have likes and commentary on their posts
> - Seeing others post comments or pictures about them that they cannot control
> - Experiencing digital FOMO, or *fear of missing out*, in which they feel they have to keep up with the latest posts on social media or else be left out the next day at school

These issues—and the behaviors and anxieties they produce—yield new challenges for modern educators to confront in the classroom. According to writer James Meikle (2012), some researchers have discovered that checking Twitter and email is harder to resist than smoking cigarettes and drinking alcohol. Others have conclusively shown that exposure to artificial light before bedtime suppresses melatonin, "resulting in a later melatonin onset in 99% of individuals and shortening melatonin duration by about 90 minutes" (Gooley et al., 2011, p. E463). The National Sleep Foundation (n.d.) finds that "reducing melatonin makes it harder to fall and stay asleep. Most Americans admit to using electronics a few nights a week within an hour before bedtime." The result is both less sleep and lower-quality rest. Students' social lives largely exist online, their use of social media is highly addictive, and they're sleeping poorly—these factors feed into and exacerbate one another, making it difficult for them to concentrate and learn in class and making school that much more peripheral to their lives.

> # NOTICE *the* WAVE
> How has the presence of smartphones directly impacted the way you teach and interact with students? Have you noticed that it takes students longer to complete assignments? Have you noticed students have a more difficult time holding a conversation or staying focused in class?

The Declining State of Student Mental Health

According to Theresa Nguyen (2017) of Mental Health America, no word describes the declining state of student mental health in the United States more appropriately than *crisis*. Let's put this crisis in its proper context: teachers' constantly expanding to-do list is stressful. The omnipotence of smartphones and the issues they breed are alarming. But the declining state of student mental health and the various psychological pathologies—such as anxiety and low self-esteem—found in virtually every classroom in America are nothing short of a matter of life and death. Tragically, this is not hyperbole. The extent of the declining state of student mental health is difficult to exaggerate.

The National Alliance on Mental Illness (2019) notes that 20 percent of Americans ages thirteen to eighteen live with a mental condition. Distressing corollaries to this epidemic include 11 percent of youth have a mood disorder, 8 percent live with an anxiety disorder, 10 percent live with a conduct disorder, and 50 percent of all lifetime cases of mental illness begin by the age of fourteen. The U.S. Department of Health and Human Services' (HHS) Office of Population Affairs (2019) adds that the "number of adolescents who experienced major depressive episodes increased by nearly a third from 2005 to 2014." A disturbing statistic from the Centers for Disease Control and Prevention (2016) tells us that in 2013 and 2014, children ages ten through fourteen were more likely to lose their lives because of suicide than because of motor vehicle accidents.

Consider the following statistics that reveal mental ailments have proliferated in both variety and intensity in fewer than ten years. Researchers Melissa C. Mercado, Kristin Holland, Ruth W. Leemis, Deborah M. Stone, and Jing Wang (2017) find that hospital admission for nonfatal self-harm among fifteen- to nineteen-year-old girls increased by well over 50 percent between the years 2009 and 2015. According to the Office of Population Affairs (2016), in 2013, 30 percent of high school students reported symptoms of depression, with female students almost twice as likely (39 percent) to report major depressive episodes as their male counterparts (21 percent). Writer Mary O'Hara (2018) finds that the sudden surge in depression and attempted suicide resulted in twice as many young people receiving hospital treatment for suicide attempts between 2008 and 2015.

How has this surge heightened the difficulties faced by everyday classroom teachers? According to the National Institute of Mental Health (2017), more than six in ten adolescents diagnosed with major depression received no treatment in 2017. Students' conditions are left largely untreated, ensuring that teachers, by their daily presence in students' lives, must confront these mental-health issues. Mental-health problems, by their very nature, are difficult to diagnose, treat, and, most of all, address in a classroom setting, as a teacher must monitor dozens of students on many fronts. But teachers often fear they are not equipped to effectively confront these complex mental-health issues, which results in more stress and tension in the classroom. Thus, a sober, honest assessment of the teaching profession's future must place declining student mental health near the top of its list of challenges.

Educational researchers have considered the extent to which smartphones and declining mental health go hand in hand, and according to journalist Brian Resnick (2019), there is considerable disagreement concerning the relationship between sudden surges in adolescent screen time and the presence of mental-health issues in youth. Do students experiencing mental-health challenges seek refuge on their phones, or does the increase in time spent on smartphones explain—to some extent, at least—the prominence of psychological problems (Resnick, 2019)?

A comprehensive study drawn from the National Survey on Drug Use and Health turned up alarming statistics on the link between social media usage and rising levels of teenage depression. According to journalist Patti Neighmond (2019), the survey took in "responses from more than 200,000 adolescents ages 12 to 17 and almost 400,000 young adults ages 18 and over between 2005 and 2017," and the study:

Found the rate of individuals reporting symptoms consistent with major depression over the past year increased 52 percent in teens and 63 percent in young adults over a decade. Girls were more vulnerable than boys. By 2017 one out of every five teenage girls had experienced major depression in the last year.

The study's chief author, Jean M. Twenge (as cited in Neighmond, 2019), believes the rise in time spent on social media plays a key role, noting that this socializing is "not as emotionally fulfilling" as face-to-face interaction. Mary Fristad (as cited in Neighmond, 2019), a clinical child psychologist, adds that spending a lot of time on social media is like "taking what happens in typical adolescent development and putting it on steroids"—that is, seeking approval, needing to fit in, and so forth, but in a space that is public and without the potential benefits of in-person contact.

Researcher Morten Tromholt (2016) shows that refraining from social media, even for a single week, can heighten well-being. Researcher Ryan Dwyer and professors Kostadin Kushlev and Elizabeth Dunn (2018) demonstrate that—perhaps unsurprising to anyone who grew up before the widespread use of such devices—the presence of smartphones significantly dampens one's enjoyment of social gatherings. Whether researchers ever come to a consensus on causation, teachers know firsthand that their students are struggling and that the concerning mental-health issues creeping into the classroom are as real as the smartphones that accompany students to school each day. The exact linkage between the two—the psychology, the technology—does not alter the reality that mental-health issues and the ubiquity of smartphones now go hand in hand.

> ## NOTICE *the* WAVE
> Have you noticed an upsurge in mental-health issues in your students in recent years? How have these problems manifested themselves in your classroom, and what manifestations do you see the most frequently (for example, anxiety, self-harm, depression, and detachment)? How has this affected you as a classroom teacher?

A Tightening Testing Regimen

Any teacher who has been in the profession since the turn of the century has experienced firsthand how the accountability movement and its emphasis on improving teacher quality have transformed education. This transformation has included a tightening testing regimen—which frequently has students take standardized tests at multiple levels of accountability (local, state, and federal)—and fundamentally added to the strain of the classroom teacher. In 2014, the National Council of Teachers of English (NCTE) produced a policy research brief that argues, "One of the effects of the increased number of heightened stakes of standardized tests is that the roles played by teachers have changed" (p. 1). Specifically, the report makes a distinction between teaching duties and institutional tasks. In addition to teaching duties, teachers must conduct the following institutional tasks.

- Collecting, organizing, and analyzing data associated with tests
- Grouping and regrouping students according to test performance
- Developing vertical articulation of the curriculum to align with tests
- Coordinating students' assignments, based on test scores, to remedial programs (NCTE, 2014, p. 1)

Institutional tasks can take anywhere from 60 to 110 hours away from instructional time per year, according to the report. Moreover, the report indicates school districts or school administrations force teachers to use materials that they did not develop and that do not even have relevance to the specific populations of the class (NCTE, 2014). Education historian Diane Ravitch (2016) argues that "if we really cared about improving the education of all students, we would give teachers the autonomy to tailor instruction to meet the needs of the children in front of them and to write their own tests." Indeed, whether the conversation is about standards and policies such as the Common Core, Race to the Top, or No Child Left Behind, opinions vary on standardized testing's value.

But high-stakes accountability has well-documented downsides that affect students and teachers alike. Millions of teachers can anecdotally confirm what professor Jennifer Jennings and research scientist Jonathan Marc Bearak (2014) find, which is that teachers frequently target their instruction to content that predictably appears on standardized exams instead of catering instruction to cultivate higher-order thinking or exposure to what is considered essential knowledge within the subject area. Also, professor Jason Grissom, associate researcher Demetra Kalogrides, and professor Susanna Loeb (2017) argue that teachers whose students receive positive test scores often get assigned to grade levels where testing occurs, usually the upper grade levels of an elementary school, leaving teachers whose students generally receive lower standardized test scores to instruct the lower grades (K–2). And perhaps most disheartening of all, David Figlio (2005), economist and dean of Northwestern University's School of Education and Social Policy, concludes that "while schools always tend to assign harsher punishments to low-performing students than to high-performing students throughout the year, this gap grows substantially during the testing window" (pp. 4–5). Students who struggle with behavioral problems receive exacerbated punishments during testing season, thus structurally incentivizing punishment in a manner that puts struggling students even farther behind.

The anxiety emanating from a culture of constant test taking manifests itself in a variety of ways. In "Fighting the Stress of Teaching to the Test," writer Stephenie Overman (n.d.) quotes Frances Banales, president of the Tucson Education Association, as saying of teachers, "Some shut down a little bit, go into automatic mode. . . . They are quieter, tense. . . . You go home exhausted. People don't eat during [periods of testing]. People try to deal with that by talking with one another." Education in the 21st century is not so much a daily process of discovery and growth but a march toward a high-stakes, climactic exam. Public officials and policymakers can debate the wisdom or folly of this transition, but this much is clear: it brings considerable pressure, anxiety, and stress into the classroom. Teachers at all phases of their careers need to learn how to prosper amid such stressful situations.

> ## NOTICE *the* WAVE
> How does high-stakes testing affect you? Does it significantly alter your classroom routine as the test gets closer? Does it affect your home life? Do you feel anxious or stressed about standardized exams, or do you handle them in a more relaxed manner?

The Violation of Perpetual School Violence

In the back of my classroom, I have two constant reminders that the era in which I teach has the potential for unspeakable horror and violence. The first item, a bucket with cat litter and a curtain in it, is needed in case a lockdown lasts so long that trapped students must go to the bathroom within the confines of the classroom. The other item is a backpack stuffed with first-aid supplies should a dire medical emergency ever present itself during the school day.

Teachers, to put it bluntly, work in an era in which they must consider the prospect of confronting incidents of gruesome violence. And students live in fear each day they go to school, knowing they could be the victims in these situations. John Woodrow Cox, Steven Rich, Allyson Chiu, John Muyskens, and Monica Ulmanu (2018) of the

Washington Post report that more than 228,000 U.S. students have experienced gun violence in schools since the mass shooting at Columbine High School in 1999. Since Columbine, violence and murder in schools has tragically become a fixed reference point on the educational landscape.

While school shootings are rare—only 10 of the United States' 135,000 schools have experienced a shooting in which there were "four or more victims and at least two deaths"—the responsibilities of teachers reflect the residual effects of events like those at Parkland, Virginia Tech, and Sandy Hook (Interlandi, 2018). Because of the public's understandable concern about school safety in the face of high-profile shootings, teachers must familiarize themselves with and master a litany of tasks and skills at the behest of districts and parents, such as how to respond to rapid school lockdowns; identify and treat acute student anxiety; instruct students on evacuation and physical threat procedures; and discuss whether to run, hide, or fight.

As with so many problems that appear in the broader social and cultural milieu, teachers feel they must steadfastly guard against future acts of violence. Psychological evaluator Ashley M. Hartz (2018) reports that teachers who took part in a survey on school gun violence and teachers' role in preventing it felt they:

> Needed to develop in students a positive social experience and guide them in a positive mindset. Participants also expressed that it is necessary to always make sure students treat each other with respect and to do the same. Participants shared the need to be vigilantly aware of their surroundings at all times. (p. 42)

However, questions and ambiguities remain: Should teachers be armed? Should teachers be able to spot would-be shooters? What are teachers' and students' roles when barricading a classroom? What should teachers do if a perpetrator attempts to enter the classroom? Should teachers sacrifice themselves for their students? The very presence of such questions in the teaching profession creates an emotional burden that communities cannot overlook or silence. Psychologically, the prospect of violence is never far from the minds of teachers or their students. Nikki Graf (2018) of the Pew Research Center reports that 57 percent of U.S. teenagers worry that a shooting could happen on their campus. And in a powerful and poignant *New York Times Magazine* exposé about teaching in the era of mass shootings, journalist Jeneen Interlandi (2018) observes:

> Teachers are at the quiet center of this recurring national horror. They are victims and ad hoc emergency workers, often with close ties to both shooter and slain and with decades-long connections to the school itself. But they are also, almost by definition, anonymous

public servants accustomed to placing students' needs above their own. And as a result, our picture of their suffering is incomplete.

School shootings are grisly and visceral because they involve both innocent children and the classroom. The classroom is supposed to be a portal to many wonderful elements of human life—learning, social interaction, and the formation of dreams. To have *this* place, of all places, targeted by violence affects teachers in a ferocious manner that we cannot ignore.

> ## NOTICE *the* WAVE
> Tragically, almost every teacher can remember a school shooting that powerfully affected him or her. Is there a specific instance of violence that changed the way you view issues of school safety? What about this particular event affected you, and how did it specifically change you as an educator?

Summary

As Shulman (2004) has indicated, classroom teaching isn't just hard work; it's "frightening" work (p. 504). It's hard to balance a never-ending to-do list in which providing emotional and academic support to each student features prominently, and this balancing act is complicated by smartphones and social media usage, which can create a barrier between students and teachers and impede learning. But it can be downright frightening for teachers to also negotiate students' declining mental health, the high-stakes-testing environment, and the threat of school violence, which teachers may feel ill equipped to handle in a manner that will best serve students and ease stress for all parties involved.

Having explored the realities of the 21st century classroom and voiced the legitimate anxieties surrounding them, in the next chapter, we'll learn strategies for addressing them head-on so that students and teachers alike can maintain a stable, nurturing classroom environment amid unpredictable occurrences and constant change.

CHAPTER 4

Promoting Learning and Mitigating Student Anxiety

The five classroom-focused strategies that follow will help you strengthen your relationship with your students as you honor their individual learning styles; make use of the technological mainstays of the 21st century; incorporate methods for coping in the classroom; mitigate the anxiety that accompanies standardized testing; and promote a calm, welcoming environment. As all classrooms differ, you may find some tips more applicable than others, and that's OK. Any of these strategies will go a long way in getting teachers and their students growing and adapting together.

Strategy 1: Teach the Student, Not the Subject

In an era in which teachers have virtually infinite responsibilities, it is essential that teachers know how to process the titanic responsibilities set before them.

Teachers cannot exhaust their long list of mandates with every student every single day. Nor should they try. Instead, teachers should approach classroom interaction in a manner that is both personal and realistically actionable. They should adopt the teaching philosophy of Sean McComb (2014), 2014 National Teacher of the Year: "kids before content." But what exactly does this mean? What does it look like when a teacher emphasizes kids before content—or teaches the student, not the content?

In practical terms, you can focus on fostering authentic relationships and acknowledging diverse student personalities by embracing the following practices.

› **Define success for students:** Teachers all define success differently, and they have diverse viewpoints about what constitutes the ultimate goal of a lesson or even an entire course. As a result, you must explain to students precisely what outcomes you want to observe and record in order to give them the best chance of reaching those outcomes. To a certain extent, there is no wrong definition of student success. Educators can debate the relative value of assessments, groupwork, writing assignments, class projects, and so on. They might disagree about techniques for delivering content, engaging in high inquiry, or encouraging collaboration. But teachers who do not clearly delineate the desired outcome of an activity (that is, explicitly define success) are much more likely to arrive at a result that is not consistent with the purpose of the lesson. Purposes, aims, and outcomes must be made explicit to students. Students, on the other hand, should know and recognize that it is always acceptable to voice confusion about the goals of a lesson or activity. Indeed, authentic classroom relationships require honesty from both parties if they are to flourish, especially in situations in which roles must be clearly understood.

> **Remember education is a process, not a product:** In 2013, TNTP conducted a survey of award-winning, celebrated teachers and found they had an array of definitions of successful teaching. Almost all their answers—from "My students are successful in future classes of the same subject" and "My students are consistently engaged in content that is intellectually challenging" to "My students go on to attend college at high rates" (TNTP, 2013, p. 8)—have one thing in common: they correctly gauge that education is not a checklist or a quantitative measure of simple success or failure. The most successful teachers conceive of their task in starkly different terms than just teaching a subject to a class. Instead, they place their class within a broader tapestry of educational experiences in which teaching an individual subject becomes not an end but merely one step in a richer process of becoming genuinely educated. Goals such as cultivating critical thought, encouraging better organization, and sparking curiosity and imagination are the by-products of a process mentality. Instruction that is embedded within a framework of such an educational process, instead of one that seeks a narrowly prescribed end, puts the focus on the student, not the teacher. To this end, a process-based philosophy of classroom interaction is one that acknowledges students' differences; different students will wish to do different things with the aptitudes they acquire in the educational process, and they will respond to the education they receive differently in both the short term and long term.

This philosophy also fosters authentic relationships as students recognize education is not a narrow pursuit but an enriching process of mental and emotional empowerment.

- **Know that support means different things to different students:** If every student had the same needs, then teaching would be more science than art. Teaching excellence would be synonymous with dynamically delivered pedagogy, and teaching would have nothing to do with personal relationships. Instead, teachers are acutely aware that each student in a classroom has his or her own talents and troubles. Effective teachers recognize the different skills and challenges of their students and see to it that they help students cultivate the former and overcome the latter. Thus, forms of support can be as diverse as the students sitting in the classroom. Support can be emotional—providing encouragement, giving timely praise or criticism, or referring a student to a counselor or intervention specialist. Support can be purely academic—helping before or after school, referring a student to supplemental materials, or reviewing previous scores and marks. Support can be as simple as making students aware that you are always happy to help, no matter what that help looks like.

- **Allow learning to wear many faces:** Instead of narrowing curricular goals, embrace the reality that authentic learning has many faces. Sometimes learning is simply listening to a lecture and taking notes. Sometimes learning is participating in specific activities or mastering a skill. As much as we teachers hate to admit it, sometimes learning can take place without any demonstrative evidence that it has taken place. Students move at different paces. Some outwardly exhibit joy in learning, while others hide their interest. Teachers mistakenly conclude that students are not learning just because they are not demonstrating their learning in the manner the teacher has asked of them. Experts, academics, and thought leaders often try to advocate for one specific form of learning over another. But teaching diverse populations necessitates that teachers allow learning to embody a variety of forms.

Strategy 2: Find the Golden Mean of Technology Teaching

Almost every teacher has wanted to scream, cry, or rage about the distraction of cell phones in the classroom. But no matter one's individual policy—"Off and away all day," "Leave the classroom if you need to use it," "Use it only for academic activities"—it would be a mistake to conclude that smartphones are always enemies of learning.

RIDE *the* WAVE
STRATEGY 1

Review the student-specific behaviors in the leftmost column that require a teacher's stepping in. For each item, list how a teacher might set the stage for a positive, productive interaction with the student. Then describe a negative interaction—or what a teacher ought not to do in that situation.

Student-Specific Behavior	Positive Student-Teacher Interaction	Negative Student-Teacher Interaction
Being habitually tardy		
Skipping classes		
Talking out of turn		
Using a cell phone		
Behaving disruptively		

Visit **go.SolutionTree.com/teacherefficacy** *for a free reproducible version of this feature box.*

While every classroom in America has been negatively transformed by both smartphones' presence and the altered social ecosystems they produce, it is unfair to conclude that smartphones cannot serve as assets. According to Nielsen (2017), "Slightly less than half (45%) of mobile kids got a service plan at 10–12 years old." And even before this age, students use tablets starting as early as first grade. Because students are so proficient (and like sponges), teachers would be wise to develop a golden mean to classroom technology usage, a mean between allowing students to recreationally stay on their devices all day and viewing 21st century technology as something that cannot help classroom teachers.

Twenty-two-year teaching veteran Ken Halla (as cited in Graham, n.d.), featured in a National Education Association article titled "Using Smartphones in the Classroom," shares four practical ideas for helping "teachers incorporate more technology and more device-based learning into their own classrooms."

1. **Ensure device use stays academic:** As difficult as it is to monitor the device usage of an entire classroom of students, you must make sure students do not use class time to update their social media posts, text their friends, or play electronic games. This will require you to be highly mobile, walking around to assess the quality of the work students complete on their devices. This will work best if assignments and activities using devices are relatively narrow and brief. Few students can resist the recreational facets of their devices for long periods. If you do not create and enforce such parameters, then devices become impediments to learning. Studies of college students have concluded that multitasking can impair students' ability to pay attention and that their use of smartphones can become, according to professor Bernard McCoy (2013), "habitual, automatic, and distracting" (p. 10). Thus, "when it comes time to get back to classroom instruction, Halla simply has the students remove their earbuds, put down their phones, and focus on what he's teaching" (Graham, n.d.).

2. **Use smartphones to keep students organized:** A benefit of students' constant engagement with their devices is it makes them easy to contact. Teachers can use a number of different applications, from Twitter to Remind, to help students stay organized and be prepared. Sending out reminders about upcoming assignments or homework that is due the next day, and even sharing a practice question or two, will allow you to have an academic presence in a digital space that is often anything but academic. Using smartphones in this way also gives parents the opportunity to follow

class activities. However, you must ensure that all communication is strictly academic in nature. With digital culture, boundaries get blurred, and it is up to you to make certain all engagement fits within professional standards and guidelines. As author and education advocate Ernest J. Zarra (2013) observes, "Teachers, who often set and meet many goals in their own lives, are often natural heroes to students. Heroes can transcend boundaries and find acceptance. However, once inside the teen's boundary, the adult has great responsibility" (p. 5).

3. **Find appropriate apps:** As of March 2018, Apple's App Store featured more than two hundred thousand apps that could be classified as education related ("Apps Announced," 2018). Any particular teacher will find the vast majority of those apps useless for one reason or another. For example, why would a first-grade teacher need an app about Advanced Placement (AP) testing, or why would a high school science teacher need an app for teaching fractions? However, the utility of apps is a promising factor in an era of endless smartphone attachment. In an article titled "Putting Education in 'Educational' Apps: Lessons From the Science of Learning," researchers argue that teachers must utilize four pillars when judging the educational merits of apps: (1) active involvement (are students at the center of whatever activity is suggested?), (2) engagement with learning materials (do the students interact with the content?), (3) meaningful experiences (how do the activity and information impact the student?), and (4) social interactions (does the app facilitate appropriate activity?) (Hirsh-Pasek et al., 2015). Lacking any of these four elements might render an app more entertaining than educational.

4. **Let fun foster productivity:** As students do work and complete tasks on their devices, allow them to stream music. As Halla observes, "It's amazing. The noise level in the classroom goes down, and the work amount goes up when you let them listen to their music" (Graham, n.d.). Additionally, if students are mature enough not to take advantage of incentives, allow them to remain on their phones after they complete their academic work, even if their phone engagement afterward becomes recreational instead of educational. This incentive can encourage students to stay focused while using technology they are already wholly comfortable with, as long as they do not rush through their work in order to recreationally use their phones. If students do rush through their work, then you should give students a limited amount of time to complete their tasks. If their music distracts students from

the moment an assignment begins, then perhaps you should not grant this privilege. Or you may wish to determine on an assignment-by-assignment basis whether music is appropriate. For example, listening to music might be better suited to working on mathematics equations rather than reading and writing exercises.

There is no ironclad policy that will always work. The bottom line is this: experiment. Try new things. Smartphones and other devices are certainly here to stay. Turning them into an asset is the surest way to successfully confront their presence in the classroom.

Strategy 3: Use Coping Strategies in the Classroom

While teachers cannot replace the knowledge and services of mental-health professionals, they can do their part in helping students cope with their emotions and behavior in a classroom setting. Mental Health America (MHA, n.d.a), a community-based nonprofit group dedicated to addressing Americans' mental-health needs and providing prevention services, offers the following highly practical tips so teachers can support those students who have difficulties managing their behavior or emotions.

- **Start fresh:** Allow yourself to form your own opinions about specific students by giving each student a fresh start to the academic year. Students change from year to year; just because a student was difficult or problematic one year does not mean that will happen again. Young people deserve as many fresh starts as possible.

- **Expect some disorganization:** Students who suffer from anxiety, or any mental-health issue, are likely to occasionally be forgetful or disorganized or experience days where they feel overwhelmed. Allow students to have occasional moments of distraction or disorganization without penalizing them too much. When students feel that their mistakes are decisive or that they can't recover from them, it acts as a potent source of anxiety. Make sure students know that their mistakes are natural and always correctable.

- **Reduce classroom stress:** Try to remove artificial barriers that lead to stress. Smile as much as possible so that students feel both welcomed into the space of the classroom and comfortable becoming members of the community that is formed in the classroom. Give students more than one day to complete homework assignments. Give students a reasonable amount of time for completing projects and preparing for exams. Remove arbitrary reasons for lowering grades that have nothing to do with academic

RIDE *the* WAVE
STRATEGY 2

Every teacher encounters specific problems with new technologies—whether it's switching over to software the school wants everyone to employ or encountering students whose device use seems to undermine classroom instruction. Write about the time in which technology most frustrated you. What happened, and what went wrong? Be sure to explain how your situation eventually got resolved.

_____
_____
_____
_____
_____
_____
_____
_____
_____
_____
_____
_____
_____
_____

*Visit **go.SolutionTree.com/teacherefficacy** for a free reproducible version of this feature box.*

performance, such as writing one's name on the wrong side of a piece of paper, demonstrating poor handwriting, or using the wrong font size. While following directions is important, enforcing them charitably helps reduce student stress and strain. You might also incorporate mindfulness apps. Writer Robyn D. Shulman (2019) reports that the most popular mindful app—Calm—is now free for teachers and students. This is an explicit recognition that teachers and students are in the midst of a mental-health crisis that requires both creativity and vigilance. As meditation expert Tamara Levitt observes (as cited in Shulman, 2019), "Teachers who practice mindfulness and meditation in the classroom commonly state that on the days when students meditate, they are calmer and accomplish more than on days without meditation."

> **Praise the good:** Most students experiencing difficulties with mental health are well aware of their flaws and weaknesses. While turning a blind eye to student shortcomings will not help, accompanying criticism with as much positive feedback and optimism as possible helps mitigate the unpleasantness of being corrected. Even failures sting less when students have reassurance that they can remedy their mistakes and that better days lie ahead. In short, give plentiful praise, especially if it can soften the reality of temporary setbacks.

> **Know how to accommodate students:** Pay close attention to individualized education plans and 504 plans, as they are usually written with the input of experts and doctors. If you have a student who you believe is experiencing stress or emotional trauma and who does not have an official plan for accommodation, suggest to the student or the parents that the school can assist in arranging such an accommodation. While it can be difficult to accommodate multiple students in multiple ways at the same time, it is well worth the effort if it removes extra anxiety from the classroom.

> **Avoid embarrassment:** When addressing a behavioral problem with a student, do it away from the rest of the class to avoid embarrassing the student. Keep the student after class, or step out into the hallway during class so that you conduct behavior modification in a private setting. Students who are argumentative, fail to follow directions, or are generally disruptive do not always know how they affect other students or the broader classroom culture. While calling out poor behavior in front of the entire class can sometimes feel cathartic for a teacher, it's dramatic, and it's

often humiliating for the student involved. Avoid student embarrassment whenever possible to help prevent the buildup of tension in a class setting.

> **Exercise compassion:** Some students face an almost-incomprehensible list of problems on a daily basis. Veteran teachers can attest they have experienced moments of utter shock when learning of the different tragedies that have befallen their students at one point or another. You cannot possibly know all the anxieties and problems students bring to school. Thus, a deep feeling of compassion for 21st century students is a powerful tool for confronting the mental-health issues plaguing them. While high standards are laudable, students often remember the teacher who went out of his or her way to smile, inquired how they were doing, had high standards but knew when to be understanding, and so forth.

> **Work with parents:** Make sure you have frequent and open dialogues with parents. This communication meets teachers' need to know of any special accommodation or situation that is not already in an individualized education plan. Maybe a traumatic event has occurred at home. Maybe a student is being bullied. Whatever the issue, teachers can better serve students when they are aware of potential sources of student distress. Likewise, teachers need to inform parents of how their children are behaving and performing in class. The public and private versions of a student are often quite different. Young people are not always the most transparent when it comes to what is happening in their classes. For students who sometimes experience anxiety, clear communication with parents is always helpful.

Strategy 4: Relax by Standardizing Standardized Tests

No matter what teachers say or do about standardized testing, this fixture of 21st century education is here to stay. But despite the stress and anxiety that these tests inevitably bring with them into the classroom, teachers and students can prosper amid this end-of-year exam process.

According to Angela Powell (2009), author of *The Cornerstone: Classroom Management That Makes Teaching More Effective, Efficient, and Enjoyable*, the key to making standardized testing a smooth and productive process is to "explain the testing situation to your students and build their self-confidence so that the process is as painless as possible" (p. 298). She suggests teachers must address four central questions for their students at different phases of the testing process, along with providing accompanying instruction and encouragement appropriate for each phase (see Powell, 2009, pp. 298–305).

RIDE *the* WAVE

STRATEGY 3

Starting at the bottom of the following pyramid, write some coping strategies that are useful in most situations. As you work your way up the pyramid, write strategies that are used less frequently in general but are especially useful in highly stressful situations. You might want to work on this with a colleague so you can brainstorm ideas together.

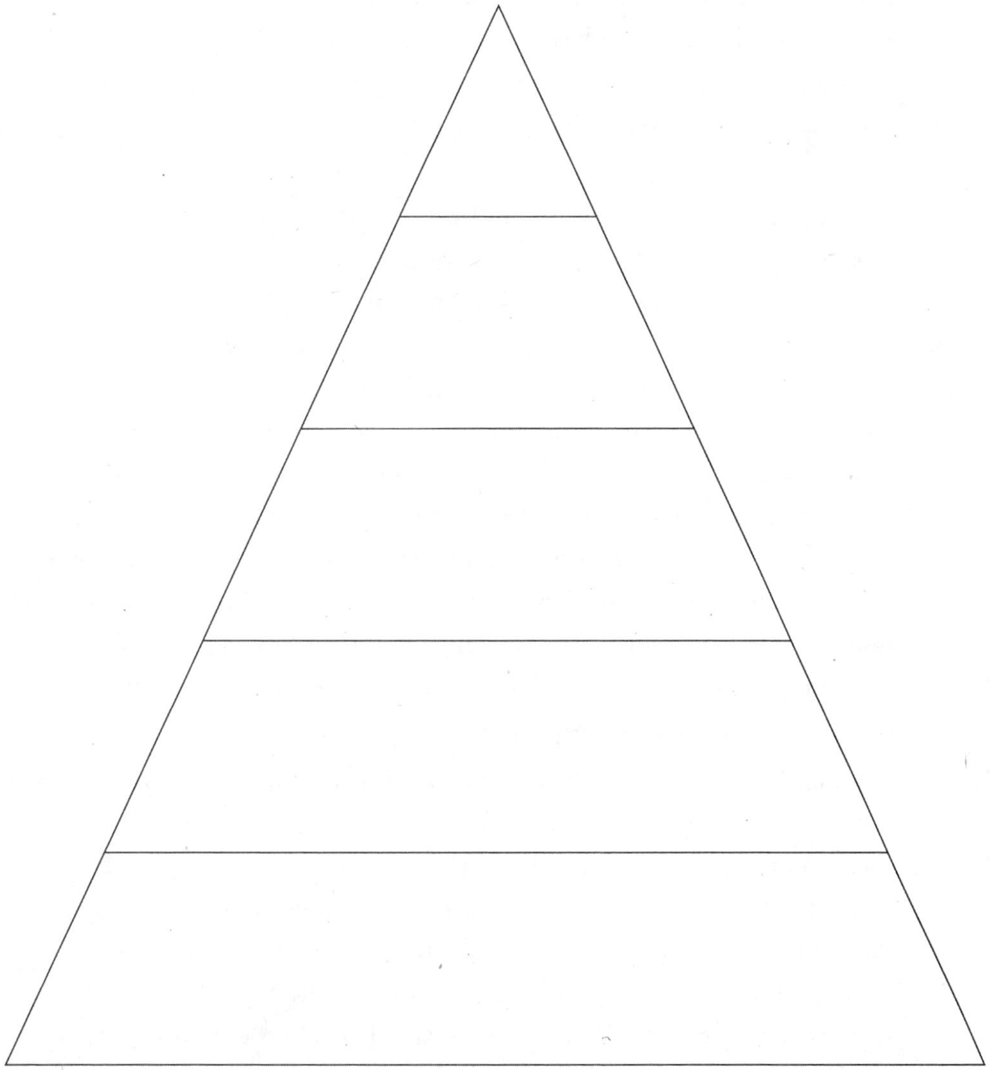

*Visit **go.SolutionTree.com/teacherefficacy** for a free reproducible version of this feature box.*

1. **Before the test, address, "Why are we doing this?":** Explain to the students that there are good reasons why they have to demonstrate what they have learned during the school year; for example, schools need to know where they are succeeding and falling short, parents need to be aware of their children's level of proficiency in various subjects, and the public has a right to know how their tax dollars are being used and to what end. Don't talk down to them by reducing standardized tests to an "adult thing" or a "politician thing." Instead, honestly state that not everybody likes these tests but that they can serve a very useful purpose in determining the successes and failures of schools and teachers. Powell (2009) describes this as "putting the test into perspective using the context of other assignments" (p. 299). In other words, this exam has a function different from those of in-class practice, quizzes, unit exams, and benchmark tests. Also, be sure to go over any vocabulary that might appear on the exam that students would otherwise not ordinarily encounter.

2. **During academic preparation, address, "Will this be on the test?":** Ensure you prepare the students well for the exams without overwhelming them with multiple-choice test questions that can drain the enjoyment from learning activities. While practice questions are a necessary step in the preparation process, you should go over incorrect answers and common mistakes without identifying the students who fell short. Stay positive as much as possible, and don't forget to give test-taking tips as a way of instilling confidence in the students. Most of all, as the school year progresses, when encountering material or activities that frequently appear on standardized tests, don't hesitate to mention that students might be tested on the material later in the year. But don't treat this material any differently than you do the rest of the course content, or else students might begin to suspect that the only important material is the tested material.

3. **During the test, address, "Can we take a break now?":** Allow the students to take as much time as possible between sessions. If the rules permit, let them eat or drink something. The most important thing is to give the students a chance to mentally recuperate. This means different things to different students. Some students want to talk to one another. Others want to sit quietly. In this era of ubiquitous devices, some will want to look at their phones to collect their wits. As the teacher, you should try to maintain a positive environment. Make a joke with the students who seem tense. Tell the students who seem discouraged that they can do it. Students will

follow the lead of the adult in the room, so model the attitude you want the students to have.

4. **After the test, address, "Is it over now?":** Let the students decompress. Sometimes, as part of decompressing, students want to discuss a few of the questions. If your state or community allows it, then let them converse. Some students want to immediately put the test behind them. If they don't want to discuss it or debrief, don't push the issue. Sometimes, teachers want to find out whether the students felt adequately prepared. Assess if the environment of the room is generally positive or negative before delving into their feelings about performance. Testing is stressful for everyone involved. The most effective teachers will try their best to adapt to the diverse responses in the aftermath of the testing period. This means catering to the needs of the students, not the adults.

Strategy 5: Aim for Pacified Teaching in a Violent Age

The drills, activities, and conversations teachers have to endure with their students are unfathomable to both retirees and outsiders to the teaching profession. Sadly, 21st century teachers have a lot of moments when they say to themselves, "I can't believe I have to do this!" Nothing evokes this sentiment quite like the reality of teaching in an era of unparalleled school violence. That said, the following actionable techniques will help quell the accompanying anxiety that so many of our students and even teachers have.

> - **Engage in honest dialogue:** Be prepared to talk to your students both *broadly* ("How do we feel, and how do we respond to the reality of school shootings in general?") and *specifically* ("How did a recent school shooting affect you?") if a mass shooting occurs in the course of the school year. The American School Counselor Association (n.d.) suggests that teachers must "be honest with kids and share with them as much information as they are developmentally able to handle." It also suggests that part of the dialogue should include an understanding that "the world is a good place to be, but that there are people who do bad things" (American School Counselor Association, n.d.). The most important thing for you to remember in these discussions is to expect the unexpected. Terror, panic, and horror arise in unpredictable ways, especially with students.

> - **Have a plan:** It's a teacher's worst nightmare, but you must explore it. In the case of an active shooter, what are your expectations as a teacher? What do you want the students to do? Depending on the students' age, are

RIDE *the* WAVE
STRATEGY 4

Write a brief letter to your state's superintendent of education telling him or her how you would like to see standardized testing reformed in your state. Make sure to explain that your opinion comes from what you have observed in your classes, and share how your experiences as a teacher inform your policy preferences.

_____
_____
_____
_____
_____
_____
_____
_____
_____
_____
_____
_____
_____
_____
_____
_____
_____
_____

*Visit **go.SolutionTree.com/teacherefficacy** for a free reproducible version of this feature box.*

Promoting Learning and Mitigating Student Anxiety

you in complete charge of protecting them, or do they have the power to choose between running and hiding? In an article from the *Atlantic* titled "Teaching While Afraid," author Ashley Lamb-Sinclair (2018) notes she spoke to fellow educators around the United States, whose school-violence approaches varied:

> Many teachers discussed the plans they've made on their own and with students, independent of school instruction. Some teachers spend time searching their classrooms for potential protective weapons, places to hide, and escape routes. An art teacher told me she had a pile of box cutters in her storage closet that she told her students was there just in case.

Each teacher will respond to a nightmare scenario differently, reflective of his or her personality, level of concern, and student population. While these individualized action plans are a contrast to the daily classroom routine, the need to create one is real, if unpleasant.

› **Reassure your students:** Instead of citing dry, detached statistics about the unlikelihood of their ever experiencing a school shooting, address students' anxiety by localizing adults' efforts to keep them safe. The Child Mind Institute (n.d.) advises teachers to "emphasize school safety" by reminding students that "school is a very safe place, filled with teachers and other adults who love [students] and have dedicated their lives to helping them." It is also helpful to remind students of all the drills and policies that the school has put in place to ensure their safety. Researchers Melissa Diliberti, Michael Jackson, and Jana Kemp (2017) find that over 95 percent of U.S. schools have procedures in place in the event of an act of violence on campus.

› **Open the door to individualized discussion:** Students might hesitate to voice their fears in class. Tell the students they are welcome to discuss their questions or concerns in a more private context. If they want to talk before or after class, make sure they know your door is always open and you are more than happy to talk about whatever questions or concerns they may have.

› **Remember communities differ:** Communities react to the reality of school shootings in a broad spectrum of ways. Some communities suggest arming teachers. Writers Kimberly Hefling and Tucker Doherty (2018) report that after Parkland, President Donald Trump suggested having retired military and law enforcement act as protectors of school sites. Other communities suggest banning firearms altogether. While teachers have a right to any and all opinions on the issue of school violence and how best to end it, be prudent when discussing the topic with students. You should be mindful that communities and even individuals within the same school site will have strong disagreements about such a personal and emotional topic. Students may well come from homes in which opinions on these matters are at variance with yours or other classroom teachers'. Tread carefully.

Summary

Every teacher in every classroom bears the pressures of constant change. Despite these 21st century struggles, teachers do wield considerable power to make the most of their situation and deliver an invaluable education to their students in the classroom. We can learn how to triumph over technology, violence, student anxiety, and other hurdles for teachers and students if we fully acknowledge these influences.

The great Roman Stoic philosopher Seneca (1918/2016), who extolled the virtues of self-mastery, eloquently writes, "He is most powerful who has power over himself." While teachers cannot control what enters their classrooms, they can control how they respond. When we approach our classroom challenges with a spirit of optimistic empowerment and involve students by nurturing a welcoming environment, we will find that we have it within ourselves to prevail and flourish in the face of adversity.

RIDE the WAVE
STRATEGY 5

Try to anticipate three responses a student might have to the following queries about how to address school shootings.

What is the plan in our individual classroom?

1.

2.

3.

When shootings occur, what are different issues that might arise for individual students processing the information?

1.

2.

3.

What are the different viewpoints adults have regarding these shootings from a political, moral, or communal standpoint?

1.

2.

3.

PART 3

colleagues

*I'm not the smartest fellow in the world, but
I can sure pick smart colleagues.*
—FRANKLIN D. ROOSEVELT

Most teachers in the state of California, where I live and work, retire somewhere between the ages of fifty-five and sixty-two because of the policies of our state retirement system. While retirement lies in my distant future—too far away to predict how I'll feel and what all will happen in the intervening years—I am certain of one thing: when the time to retire eventually arrives, I will desperately miss my friends on staff. Many of my colleagues serve as sentimental fixtures of a meaningful career. To say goodbye to them—either when I retire or when they do—will be no easy task.

Since 2001, my social studies department has gone to the movies after the first day of finals every December. Every year, we try to list all the films we have watched together over the decades. Sometimes the films are great (*The Blind Side* and *Life of Pi*). Sometimes they aren't. I still get mercilessly teased for having suggested gems such as *The Tourist*, *The Day the Earth Stood Still*, and *Exodus: Gods and Kings*. On the first day of finals in the spring, we always go out to a department luncheon, usually Basque food. We have organized baby showers for one another and gone to the weddings of one another's children. And yes, sometimes we fight. Once, in the middle of an election season, two stalwarts of the department got into a ferocious fight that upset everyone in the room. But as with arguments among family members, eventually everyone moved on.

Before they enter the classroom for the first time, few teachers are aware of just how potent and resplendent the camaraderie among teachers can be. I suspect that if teachers had to list their best friends (not including spouses), chances are many would mention fellow teachers.

Most of the time, an individual teacher can explain why he or she is stressed or burned out. Teachers can explain why they are frustrated with their students, their administrators, and the negative press they frequently endure from the community. But human friendships are different—enigmatic and fraught with complexity. Teachers have to understand why relationships between and among colleagues can become strained in an era of reform and change if those relationships are to flourish. Most important, teachers should learn what to do when the markings of strain appear in their staff relationships, when department or staff morale begins to wane, and when hostility replaces camaraderie.

The strong, supportive relationships we build with our colleagues help keep us from being flattened by the waves of constant change and reform, so anything that affects these relationships should be taken seriously. This is a universal truth, regardless of where teacher relationships are formed. Julie A. Gray and Robert Summers (2015) conducted a study investigating "the role of enabling school structures . . . collegial trust, and collective efficacy in 15 pre-Kindergarten to 12th grade international, private schools in South and Central America" (p. 61). Their conclusion was not surprising: they found that "certain physical and structural conditions must be developed for a PLC to exist and be sustained over time" (Gray & Summers, 2015, p. 71).

Thus, the workplace has a decisive role in how much people thrive or struggle. Teachers have relationships that run the gamut from best friend to nodding acquaintance in the copy room and everything in between. Wherever colleagues fall on the continuum, school sites thrive when these relationships are marked by deep respect, civility, and a willingness to see one another as coequals. These qualities encourage a space for mentoring, sharing ideas, and challenging one another in ways that improve teacher efficacy. And in an era of constant change and reform, such healthy relationships among colleagues can be imperiled.

CHAPTER 5

Unraveling the Conflict Among Teachers

Constant change affects not only individual teachers and the classrooms where they spend their days but also the relationships that teachers have with one another. Much has been written about professional norms, professional learning communities (PLCs), and the types of interactions teachers have as colleagues teaching on the same campus—in both a professional context (for example, attending meetings and engaging in professional development) and more convivial activities (for example, eating lunch together, chaperoning school dances, and going to sporting events). But perhaps the most underreported element of this fluctuating profession is the pressure it places on all these relationships between and among colleagues—and how it can affect these relational dynamics on a school campus.

Teaching veterans can attest to the power these staff relationships have in our lives. Our colleagues are often our best friends. They understand our travails and our grievances. They share our language of hope and discontent because they live their lives at a similar pace. The very calendar of our lives is the same—vacations, workdays, and the stresses of the conventional school year are concurrent, for better or for worse.

The teachers' lounge is both a literal place where teachers gather and a timeless metaphor to describe the gathering of professionals who all feel the brunt of changing expectations. As a child of two teachers, I spent my nights listening to my parents banter about their fellow staff at the dinner table. Sometimes, the stories were complimentary in nature, though often they were not, but there was never any question that the human beings who populated the school staff intimately affected my parents' work and well-being.

In my career, I have witnessed colleagues fall in love and marry. I have watched teachers become best friends, and I know that some staff vacation or spend weekends together. I have also watched some friendships become toxic and others slowly decline as two people merely grow apart. I have seen cliques form and then dissolve. I have observed fellow staff scream at one another—about politics, of course—and then renew their fraternal bond when election season ends.

Sometimes, colleagues are the ones who lift us up during our darkest hours, when emotional, physical, and relational fortitude fail us. They are present for divorces, illnesses, and funerals. Author and historian Kate Bowler (2018) tells of the joy she derived from the prayers of her fellow Duke Divinity staff as she underwent surgery to treat stage IV colon cancer:

> It pleases me to no end to find out later that the most serious scholars I have ever known—authors of weighty books and owners of many velvet smoking jackets—have cried snotty tears as they pleaded with God to extend my life. They are teaching me the first lesson of my new cancer life—the first thing to go is pride. (p. 55)

These relationships with our colleagues matter—they matter a lot. And they are greatly affected by the titanic changes we endure in our era of teaching. In an effort to understand the full weight of the stress and strain these relationships are subjected to, we'll look at how teachers are spending less spontaneous, unstructured time with one another. We'll also consider the ways in which professional development can actually rupture relationships between different generations of teachers; how accountability measures can spark jealousies; and why teachers often feel they must choose between maintaining a colleague's friendship and adhering to the highest professional standards.

The Echo in Teachers' Cafeterias

When I first started teaching in 1998, the teachers' lounge bristled with noise and frenetic activity at lunchtime. Microwaves beeped, refrigerator doors opened and closed, and colleagues conversed about everything imaginable. Even then, those of similar generations congregated—new teachers ate lunch at one table, the veterans ate at another—yet groups were always well within earshot of each other, so the veterans could offer their sage-like wisdom to the novices on staff.

One of my most vivid memories of being a new teacher is having a hearty group of veterans put down their lunches to teach me how to properly break up a fight. I had failed miserably on my first attempt. I'd walked right into the middle of a freshman melee and promptly gotten punched, leaving me with a rather embarrassing black eye and rumors swirling on campus that I had "gotten beat up by a freshman."

Despite our widely divergent levels of classroom experience, we had a mutual understanding; we were all on the same page, proud members of the profession, proud teachers of a school we adored, and proud participants in the noble cause of educating students. This was long before my colleagues and I would come to know well the phrase *professional learning community*. These memories from the beginning of my career stand as a totem of what camaraderie feels like, what it looks like to gather and share, and how we might teach classes on our own but know that we always have help close at hand.

In 2020, when I visit the teachers' lounge during lunch, it is eerily quiet and virtually vacant; there are no loud conversations, and the couches along the far wall are almost always empty. A short walk to the teachers' cafeteria reveals a similarly isolating scene. Ironically, in an era when educators champion cooperation and channel resources and time into cultivating collaboration as a central tenet of teacher professionalism, teachers are experiencing new and challenging chasms as their responsibilities pile up, such as disagreement about new teaching modalities that districts and state governments implement, as well as the wisdom of attempting to act as a counselor when teachers address issues of stress, anxiety, and depression. Researchers Matthew Ronfeldt, Susanna Owens Farmer, Kiel McQueen, and Jason Grissom (2015) report that 84 percent of teachers work in collaborative groups and 90 percent of those teachers say they find the collaboration helpful to their professional behavior. Thus, the problem is not that teachers don't collaborate or don't find value in their collaborative time together. The problem is that this collaboration is less organic, less spontaneously constituted, than it once was.

A voluminous body of research confirms the utility and benefit of building collaborative time into teachers' work schedules. In a doctoral dissertation study, Tami Burton (2015) explains how well this has been established in recent years:

> Teacher collaboration is not a new topic. In fact, this topic is related to several previous studies. Goddard and Goddard (2007) conducted a similar study on teacher collaboration and student achievement. Their findings suggest that when teachers engage in high levels of collaboration, student achievement is enhanced. Collaborating teams assist in creating small learning communities within the school (Main & Bryer, 2003). (p. 72)

This much is beyond dispute. Yet the professional arsenal of 21st century teachers lacks more traditional staff cohesion. To have this cohesion, teachers need a natural gathering where the free interplay of ideas is conditioned not by "PLC time," learning teams, and the like but through associative activities like eating meals together and congregating in the office before the school day begins. Sadly, teachers sacrifice these spontaneous meetups as they stay in their rooms at lunch or rush to their classrooms first thing in the morning to tick off items on their growing list of responsibilities—conducting an intervention with a struggling student, making sure a bullied student has a safe place to eat lunch, answering emails, returning parent phone calls, and so on. Teachers' days are so packed with independent tasks that it's difficult for teachers to coordinate or set aside any time for collaboration—let alone hope they will run into each other accidently so that they may be able to organically bounce ideas off each other in the manner that they might during their (often nonexistent) lunchtime. This is exactly what journalist and teacher Sara Mosle (2014) finds in schools attempting to launch voluntary pilot programs:

> An administrator introduced lesson study as part of the staff's professional development at a school where I've worked. There was just one problem: we teachers—juggling tutoring before and after school, supervising clubs, or coaching sports—had only one period a week to meet as a group. It would be generous to say lesson study didn't work; it never got off the ground. There typically isn't time in American teachers' workdays for this kind of collaborative enterprise.

Teachers need to connect with one another because, as authors Claire Kaplan, Roy Chan, David A. Farbman, and Ami Novoryta (2015) state, they are on "the frontlines of both unpacking and applying the new standards, teachers are becoming the experts, and they learn both from and with one another" (p. 67). These surges in professional growth—unpacking standards, sharing forms of expertise, engaging in small talk about whatever is a hot topic on campus—require time and space that is not always clearly delineated by meetings, workshops, or trainings. Sometimes this growth takes place in the copy room while one teacher waits for another teacher to finish a print job. Maybe it's talking to a classroom neighbor between periods. Maybe it is seeing a colleague off campus and starting up a conversation about mutual concerns, whatever those may be. Unfortunately, teachers clearly lack the time to informally converse and socialize. As Jennifer Davis (2015) at *Education Week* observes:

> Teachers have just a few minutes a day for collaborative work. The reasons for this dearth are simple: Time for collaborative teacher development has not been a priority, and the standard school schedule allows little time for teachers to meet during the day.

Solving this problem is complicated—Does the school day need to lengthen so teachers have longer lunches? Should a new educational schedule build in more non-teaching time before and after students are on campus so teachers can attend to all the responsibilities now placed on them?

Finland has long been hailed as a kind of holy grail for school reform and a model for educational success. Skeptics might point out that Finland is a small homogeneous nation with a different form of government, less poverty and inequality, and a culture that champions teaching as a career. But no matter where one stands on the question of why Finnish schools are so successful, there is no quibbling with its sterling Programme for International Student Assessment, or PISA, scores. The National Center on Education and the Economy (n.d.) points out that Finnish teachers set aside considerable professional development time, organized by both teachers and the administration:

> Research indicates that the average Finnish teacher spends seven days a year on professional development, with some municipalities arranging large, multi-school training events and others leaving it up to schools to develop in-service programs. However, teachers' schedules in Finland enable a great deal of teacher collaboration to support their professional growth. The school day allows time for planning, collaborating, and meeting with other teachers to discuss challenges or successes, and other professional work, such as reading and doing research, and most schools do this.

Unlike nations that set aside time for teachers, we cannot take it for granted that new pressures that ask more of teachers will spawn habits among colleagues—after all, teachers at all stages of their careers need support from one another. As authors Richard DuFour and Michael Fullan (2013) observe in *Cultures Built to Last: Systemic PLCs at Work*®:

> When the PLC process drives an entire system, participants come to have a sense of identity that goes beyond just their own piece of the system. They identify in palpable ways with the overall organization, unleashing the energy of mutual allegiance and competition for the common good. This "systemness" exists in the hearts and minds of the people working together for the betterment of the system and is a defining characteristic of the culture. (p. 3)

The echo in cafeterias, lounges, and break rooms is not a disease. It is a symptom of a much bigger problem that needs addressing—chiefly, that less unstructured time results in fewer personal connections, which makes teachers feel they are alone in their profession, even when they are officially functioning as collaborative teams. At its core, what is at stake is nothing less than a consideration of the question that finds its roots in every human profession: How do practitioners of education honor their commitments within a dynamic and fast-changing profession without forfeiting the traditional human relationships that facilitate professional success?

> ## NOTICE *the* WAVE
> Do you find value in spending time with colleagues that is not strictly prescribed collaborative group time? Has your ability to spend time with colleagues during the school day changed over the years?

Generational Chasms in Professional Development

Professional development can act as a source of tension between colleagues during times of constant disruption and change. This is because teachers, at different points in their careers, may have divergent reactions to professional development that encourages them to broadly change specific facets of their teaching repertoire. Teachers often perceive sudden and drastic changes in education differently depending on whether they are new or experienced.

Teachers with years of experience tend to approach the newest teaching initiative or trend with heightened skepticism, for a good reason: frequently in the course of a career, a teacher will dramatically change his or her teaching, curriculum, expectations, or procedures only to be told that he or she must reinvent the proverbial wheel once again a few years later. When a teacher has been in the profession long enough, he or she sees trends often have a cyclical flow and come in and out of fashion—over the course of decades. Author Peg Grafwallner (2017) notices that:

> Veteran teachers are highly experienced, having seen every "new" initiative of education. They know a recycled idea when they hear one. They remember when *differentiated instruction* meant a child's individual learning style, *backward design* meant writing the test first, and *higher order thinking skills* meant there could be more than one right answer.

While young teachers frequently approach new trends and policies with a more open and welcoming—even enthusiastic—disposition, veterans are wary of this level of change. The varied viewpoints often make for awkward moments during professional development activities. New teachers, in the dawn of their respective careers, eagerly oblige and are already in a mode of getting on board, whereas their older cohorts, many of whom have been tenured for decades, do not so eagerly embrace the latest trend or endorse the newest fad. Increasingly, administrators and teacher leaders are realizing that this breeds tension between generations of teachers.

In the aftermath of trainings, workshops, and professional development days, the schism between novice and veteran is vast. Despite the $18 billion that is spent annually on professional development in the United States, with teachers typically spending sixty-eight hours engaged in these activities, very few teachers (29 percent) "are highly satisfied with current professional development offerings" (K–12 Education Team, 2015, p. 3).

This dissatisfaction has diverse causes. But it may in part come from the flattening and homogenizing effect professional development can unintentionally have when teachers do not receive differentiated trainings at different points in their careers. As Roger Vanderhye (2015), principal of Spring Hill Elementary School in McLean, Virginia, astutely observes:

> Professional development for veteran teachers needs to be individualized. Teachers with a rich background of experience, training, and knowledge need to be treated the way one would treat a specialized surgeon: update their training only in the areas of need. (p. 40)

Indeed, most trainings for teachers are viewed "more as a compliance exercise than a learning activity" (K–12 Education Team, 2015, p. 10). Only 30 percent of teachers report that they have ever had a choice of professional development activities, and 18 percent have never had the opportunity to provide input on the forms of training they receive (K–12 Education Team, 2015).

NOTICE *the* WAVE

Do you notice a difference in how new and experienced teachers react to professional development activities—specifically when trainings push a paradigm shift in instruction, curriculum, or technology? If so, how are these differences manifested, and in what contexts do they occur? How can professional development experiences become more personalized to account for the reality that teachers are at different points in their careers?

Jealousies and Juxtapositions in an Era of Accountability

A variety of new pressures, reforms, and technologies in education have contributed to a community in which teachers sometimes find themselves at odds with one another. Tension between teaching colleagues is not new. In any profession, human beings who day after day work in close proximity, deal with high-pressure situations, and face expanding expectations naturally experience tension and disagreement. A little competition between colleagues can foster innovation, bring about better outcomes, and make the individuals work harder than what their job usually requires or calls for. But in an era of pressure to create new and relevant curricula, teacher accountability, intense high-stakes testing, and teacher social media use, competition can turn toxic.

In this era that emphasizes developing new lessons and curricula and adjusting old ways of delivering information to comport with the latest technologies, there is the phenomenon of the "show-off" teacher. Professional jealousy among teachers is sometimes most potent when one teacher decides to demonstrate new materials and methods with great fanfare and aplomb. Instructional designer Natalie Laderas-Kilkenny (2007) relates the experience of attending an education conference and hearing teachers denigrate other teachers who were eager and creative, which she attributes to the former group's own insecurities. Laderas-Kilkenny (2007) writes of some of the participants' negativity:

> It actually reminded me of an attitude I'd seen among teachers. There really was this feeling that spread in the faculty lounge that it was not okay to be a "show off." "Show offs" included people who used new and different teaching styles and approaches or people who "stood out" as teachers. "Show offs" were not to be trusted and often there were political struggles within the school where the "show offs" were involved.

Of course, this tension has two sides to it. On one side are the innovative teachers who feel that they are merely doing what they are supposed to do. On the other side are their colleagues, who experience the annoyance of observing a teacher behave in a manner they consider ostentatious. No matter which side a teacher comes down on, tension is sure to be present.

Adding to this tension is an increase in accountability measures, which often lead to teachers' comparing themselves to one another. In an environment in which data, scores, and benchmarks decide the quality of instruction that a classroom offers, sometimes teachers do not want to share their strategies or curricula with others. Instructional coach Janet Allen (2015) writes in an article titled "When Teachers Compete, No One Wins" that she has:

> Taught and coached at schools where the animosity between teachers is palpable. Individuals who are otherwise truly great teachers

spitefully refuse to help each other or collaborate because of a variety of perceived slights, rumors, and personal judgments. They jealously guard their best lessons and strategies, convinced that their colleagues don't deserve to benefit from them.

While it might sound as though the teachers are behaving like the students, a striking source of jealousy among teachers stems from social media usage. Teachers who engage in social media activity sometimes inadvertently sow division because of their perceived successes on different platforms. Writer Janelle Cox (n.d.) observes:

> With teachers that work so closely together, it can get quite uncomfortable. In today's education system, many teachers use social media. This allows teachers to share photographs of their ingenious and creative lesson plans with their fellow teachers. With this may come some jealousy and insecurity in others, because those teachers who aren't as talented may feel like less of a teacher.

And whether or not social media is involved, by and large, teachers do not enjoy having to market their own successes or to act as educational PR agents highlighting classroom successes. Researcher Izhar Oplatka (2006) finds that doing so is often associated with exceedingly high levels of stress. Yet teachers frequently encounter situations where they must demonstrate their own successes or worthiness as educators. Teachers who are in charge of academic programs must sometimes compete with supervisors of other programs on campus in order to attract the most capable students. Even more dismaying is the fact that, online, school sites are given star ratings, akin to those that movies or restaurants receive. In these digital forums, anyone can anonymously comment on individual teachers for any reason. It should come as no surprise that in such an environment, there may be rivalries, jealousies, and tension among teachers.

NOTICE *the* WAVE

In your time as a professional educator, have you ever observed or experienced conflict with a colleague because he or she refused to share materials or advice with other teachers? Is it ever appropriate to withhold assistance to other staff members? What do you think are the main drivers of conflict between teachers on a school campus, and do any of these drivers differ from those that were pervasive earlier in your career?

Good Friend, Poor Colleague or Good Colleague, Poor Friend

Every teacher knows this awkward situation well: you are friends with colleagues who are not being the best teachers they can be. Maybe they feel burned out. Maybe they won't admit that their practices are not particularly effective. Maybe they are simply being lazy. Maybe they are so complacent in their jobs that their failure doesn't register. Sometimes, your friends might even seem to relish indifference or mediocrity.

You want to say something, but you worry your friendships will suffer if you do. After all, you might eat lunch with these colleagues or spend occasional weekends and holidays with them. And, most difficult of all, you think they are high-quality human beings. They are loyal spouses and loving parents, and they contribute to your community in meaningful and impactful ways. At one time, they might have been highly effective classroom teachers. All these reasons explain your hesitancy to step in and offer even the faintest form of criticism or seek the smallest amount of accountability.

You may even express frustration at this expectation that you monitor your colleagues. After all, why is it your responsibility to say anything? You wonder, "Isn't this what administrators are supposed to be doing?"

A number of pressures and expectations of 21st century teaching force educators into this uncomfortable situation.

First, teachers work in an era where they are judged, fairly or not, by the overall school's performance on standardized exams. While this can be a significant vehicle and incentive for cultivating collaboration and teamwork, it also transfers difficult burdens to teachers who are aware of struggling or unprofessional colleagues. This makes for a tricky dynamic in which the desire to be a school that performs well on standardized exams can imperil friendships. The National Education Association (2015) reports that teachers who feel pressure from their peers, as well as from others, are more likely to report that "standardized testing has a negative impact on their classrooms," "they spend too much time on standardized testing," and "their evaluations depend to a moderate or extreme degree on student test scores" (p. 1). These findings confirm that uncomfortable but inevitable sentiments may emerge: Why should a staff's reputation be jeopardized by a few teachers? What has priority—community outcomes or individual relationships?

A second element that spawns the dichotomy between friendship and professionalism is the emphasis on accountability through transparency. Researcher Brian Gill (2017) argues that:

> One of the hallmarks of professional accountability is transparency of practice, which induces accountability through (at least) the mere presence of another. Improving the rigor and utility of observations of classroom practice has been the most prominent method of promoting professional accountability through transparency over the last few years.

While transparency and accountability are undeniably positive features of any professional community, the personal and the professional naturally blur when a colleague and friend holds the line on professional standards. Negotiating the interests of students, who will graduate or move on in the short term, and the interests of a friend, who is a more permanent fixture in a colleague's life, can create a difficult—and sometimes excruciating—situation for a teacher.

Finally, the dichotomy between friendship and professionalism often arises when exemplary teachers are asked to be team leaders of professional learning communities. Authors Robert Eaker and Janel Keating (2009) explain team leaders' responsibilities, which sometimes include communicating professional development needs to fellow team members:

> Team leaders are expected to enhance the capacity of their team to work interdependently to achieve common goals. . . . In fulfilling the role of leading their team, team leaders are responsible for such functions as leading the team in preparing and utilizing team norms, planning agendas, chairing meetings, serving as a direct communications link between the administration and the faculty, leading the work of teams in analyzing and improving student learning data, seeking out and experimenting with best practices, leading the collaborative development and attainment of learning improvement goals, and identifying and communicating professional development needs.

Team leaders occupy a unique space in the ecosystem of education. They are not administrators, they have no power to discipline or enforce rules and regulations, and their job descriptions do not differ from those of anyone else in their department or school. Yet they are sometimes tasked with not only modeling effective classroom practices but also communicating issues to other members of their PLC "for which team members hold themselves *mutually accountable*" (Eaker & Keating, 2009). Hence, team leaders find themselves on the horns of a dilemma: Should they be good friends (who know their place) or good colleagues (who look out for the broader interests of the school and the students)? There are no easy answers; clearly, this is a genuine and persistent source of strain in the relationships between and among colleagues.

> # NOTICE *the* WAVE
>
> Have you ever felt torn between loyalty to a friend and loyalty to your school? What was the issue, and how did it eventually get resolved? When do you think it is appropriate to voice a professional concern or disapproval to a colleague who you also consider a friend? How would you respond to a friend criticizing you about something related to your professional behavior?

Summary

In his groundbreaking social science book *Bowling Alone: The Collapse and Revival of American Community*, which holds up with passing years, Robert Putnam (2000) observes that although people still bowl, they now do it alone instead of in leagues. Putnam (2000) makes this observation as part of a larger assertion that Americans are participating less in social groups, which is consistent with what I have witnessed in teachers' lounges and staff cafeterias over the course of my career. The weakening bonds on a school campus and the disintegration of bowling leagues appear to be manifestations of a single growing trend, but the situation in education has especially alarming ramifications for teachers and, by extension, their students—those who will carry us into the future.

In the next chapter, we'll look at specific ways to ease the mounting strains associated with these weakened bonds so that the strains no longer interfere with teachers' ability to really connect with one another personally and professionally. With the next chapter's strategies, teachers can ultimately enliven their day-to-day work and dramatically transform the way they educate.

CHAPTER 6

Committing to Teacher Collaboration

As you move from the classroom sphere to the space you inhabit with your colleagues, you'll naturally take with you some fundamentals of interaction—practicing kindness, recognizing the individual, being cheerful, and showing that you want to be there. But the five strategies that follow focus on true collaboration with the teachers at your school. You'll discover just how much you can gain—individually and collectively—by treating your colleagues like fellow citizens, seeking out mentorships, borrowing ideas from peers, understanding and demonstrating your connection to other teachers and their contributions, and uniting through your common calling to tackle larger initiatives.

Strategy 1: Create an Admirable Miniature Body Politic

Since 1998, I have taught high school and college civics to students from every background imaginable. After two decades on the journey of a teacher, I have concluded that schools are microcosms of the larger society and culture. Generally, when educators make this observation, they are saying that social trends and cultural markings have an effect on the classroom, which is undeniably true. But I mean something very different by *microcosm*. I mean that the structure, function, and membership of a school are remarkably similar to those of society writ large.

Schools have rules, some of which they create and some of which they don't. Schools have leaders, but these leaders have limited powers. Schools have policies, but these are always in flux and being negotiated by stakeholders. Schools have their own traditions and important events. This sounds similar to virtually every community because schools are a miniature body politic: they rise and fall, flourish and flounder on the basis of their citizens' behavior.

Students quickly come and go. Administrators often don't last very long. In an era of frequent upheaval, the teachers are the pillars of the school community and endure the constancy of change together. Staff cohesion and high morale, then, are critical. As writer and school administrator Derrick Meador (2018) rightly observes, "Education is a highly difficult concept for those outside the field to understand. Having peers that you can collaborate with and lean on during tough times is essential." Meador (2018) makes the following suggestions that will help teachers build a strong sense of solidarity and ensure the body politic of the school thrives in turbulent times.

> **Show kindness and humility:** Go out of your way to highlight the success of other classes, programs, and teachers. A spotlight is a powerful thing, and aiming it first at your colleagues' success instead of your own achievements cultivates goodwill.

> **Be happy:** While this might sound a bit trivial, the power of a smile and a positive demeanor is undeniable. Happy teachers in a learning community are like rays of sunshine to trees—others will bend and stretch to absorb the light. While being happy is not always easy, teachers should do their best to curb genuine feelings of negativity, anxiety, and distress over the course of a school year.

> **Resist gossip:** To put it simply, gossip is the nuclear bomb of staff morale, especially for a small staff. Avoid it at all costs.

> **Let colleagues' undue commentary roll off your back:** You cannot control what other staff do or say about you. When you hear unfair criticism or unprofessional comments directed your way, try your best to shrug them off. Don't let others determine your value as an educator.

> **Collaborate with your peers:** Here, a teacher encountering new problems or digesting what the next reform will require of him or her can find both support and strength. Teachers encounter change together on a school campus. Verbalize worries and concerns. Formulate a strategy for dealing with them. Absorb the ideas and experiences of others. Collaborating with your peers can ease all facets of a constantly changing campus.

> **Watch what you say to people:** When citizens bemoan a culture in decline, they often highlight the unpleasantness of people's public behavior—the vulgarity, the absence of basic manners, the hollowness

of everyday interaction. Be as pleasant as possible. Speak genuinely, but also try to focus on the positive when talking to fellow members of your teaching community.

> **Keep your promises:** Your fellow teachers sometimes need your help—maybe they need help developing curriculum, collaborating on a campus project, or driving a van to a sporting event. Whatever it is, make sure you always follow through on your promises. Colleagues who are pillars of respect always do so. Be like them.

> **Learn about others' outside interests:** Communities work when their members feel valued. Learning about a fellow teacher's outside interests shows that you view him or her as more than just a colleague; you understand that he or she is an entire human being with interests, hobbies, and struggles beyond the school community. If you want others to feel valued not just as teachers but as individuals, inquire about elements of life unrelated to their working lives.

> **Be open minded:** Communicating through certitudes is not just futile and unpleasant; it's bad politics. There is a reason why wisdom is not synonymous with verbosity. Listen more than you talk. Assume that you don't know everything. And, most of all, realize that acknowledging someone else has good ideas does not make your ideas bad. Avoid the obstinacy that comes with thinking open-mindedness signifies weakness, as it closes a teacher off to an entire universe of possibilities.

> **Remember that some feelings are hurt more easily than others:** We've all done it before—made a joke that someone interpreted in a way we had not intended. Get to know your colleagues before making biting, edgy, or sarcastic comments. The rules of verbal discourse are perpetually fluid. Know the lay of the land before you venture too far.

> **Don't worry about accolades:** Teaching is the wrong profession for those seeking fame, fortune, or trophies. Instead of focusing on those things, remember why you became a teacher, and do the right thing as much as humanly possible. Teachers who focus on student achievement—and not necessarily their own achievement—will find solidarity, camaraderie, and cohesion among fellow staff members.

RIDE the WAVE
STRATEGY 1

Derrick Meador (2018) suggests the following practices for building an admirable miniature body politic. Place a check mark next to those that you use or have used as an educator, and explain how you've carried them out. Place an X next to the practices that you don't use but would like to use in the future, and explain how you might incorporate them into your work life.

Practice for Building an Admirable Miniature Body Politic		Explanation
Show kindness and humility.		
Be happy.		
Resist gossip.		
Let colleagues' undue commentary roll off your back.		
Collaborate with your peers.		
Watch what you say to people.		
Keep your promises.		
Learn about others' outside interests.		
Be open minded.		
Remember that some feelings are hurt more easily than others.		
Don't worry about accolades.		

Source: Adapted from Meador, D. (2018, July 9). The importance of effective communication between teachers. Accessed at www.thoughtco.com/the-importance-of-effective-teacher-to-teacher-communication-3194691 on July 17, 2019.

Visit **go.SolutionTree.com/teacherefficacy** *for a free reproducible version of this feature box.*

Strategy 2: Seek Wise Mentors and Impressionable Mentees

In my third year of teaching, a student in my freshman world history class was the daughter of a legendary college professor from my community. Upon hearing that I'd once played college tennis, she suggested I play with her father, who was almost three decades my senior but still a more-than-proficient tennis player. Thus began the most powerful mentoring relationship in my life and career.

For the next decade, our routine was simple: every few months, we would play two sets of tennis and then retire to the clubhouse, where we would eat lunch and discuss everything under the sun—books, teaching, parenthood, writing, and so on. I was in the infancy of my career, with no children at home and only the faintest dream of writing books that would—hopefully—make a difference to those who read them. Meanwhile, he had secured his status as a much-beloved teacher long before, and he had a sterling reputation as a scholar of Shakespeare. As I look back on our conversations, I couldn't possibly quantify his insights about the splendor of a life spent teaching and writing. But I am certain that had I not experienced his friendship and mentoring, my life would not be as rich and satisfying as it is today.

The relationships we have with fellow educators can affect educational outcomes just as our relationships with students do. Specifically, if we mentor younger teachers while simultaneously gaining mentorship from teachers we aspire to be like, it can greatly improve students' learning. Authors Ellen Moir, Dara Barlin, Janet Gless, and Jan Miles (2009) explain that:

> Much as the classroom teacher has been shown to be the single most important ingredient in student learning, the mentor is the most critical element in an effective mentoring program. No matter which model is used or which management structure is provided, if the mentors in a program are outstanding, the program will be outstanding and new teachers will have the opportunity to reflect meaningfully on their practice and accelerate their instructional growth. (p. 32)

Classroom teachers don't always think about this dynamic, yet my own mentor helped me hone my skills so I could better teach all my students.

There are dozens of mentoring programs in virtually every state in America. They all have their own structures, aims, and procedures, but most of them promote conventional mentoring relationships. Conventional mentoring relationships are intensely practical, generally focusing on school procedures, pedagogy, or certain tenets of teaching professionalism. And this is nothing to bemoan. But in an era of constant change, we need a qualitatively different type of mentoring relationship—one that is rooted not in procedure and paperwork but in passion and purpose. The type of mentor who will most benefit teachers battling constant change encourages teachers, both novices and hardened veterans, to foster a deeper, more broadly reflective approach to education as a lifelong profession. As teaching changes and gets harder, finding a mentor who helps you transcend the myopia of the moment, or to see the forest and the trees, will pay dividends. Marcy Whitebook, director of the Center for the Study of Child Care Employment, and coauthor Dan Bellm (2014) note:

> Historically, mentoring has been thought of as a strategy to support new teachers, often within the context of their pursuit of higher education, but mentoring now takes place in a wider range of settings, with variations in mentoring goals and mentor-protégé relationships. (p. 14)

Variations in the mentor relationship can empower teachers to develop more long-term goals than what traditional mentoring programs require, consider what their individual aims may be, and formulate notions of identity that transcend curriculum-oriented teacher functions. Mentors can stoke passion and help teachers identify purpose and better define how they wish to be remembered by students, rather than focus on their effectiveness in terms of raw data.

Thus, it is important to keep in mind the following general guidelines as you consider entering into a more organic and unconventional mentorship.

› **Find someone who has what you want:** If you want to become the superintendent of your school district, then reach out to the current superintendent. If you want to become a teaching coach, a union rep, or a writer of education books, find people in your community who are doing what you eventually want to do. You will always feel pressure—both internally and externally—to conform your teaching habits and aims to the trend of the moment. After all, good teachers know they are accountable to administrators and the districts they teach in. Still, teachers should find a way to think long term and choose someone who has already arrived at the destination they seek. Not only will this impart some wisdom, but it will also offer you what the 21st century teacher's career arc often lacks—career ladders and new possibilities.

› **Reach up, not out:** Don't be afraid to make contact with someone who is clearly more accomplished than you are. Of course, every journey or career is distinctive. But merely commiserating with peers rarely delivers the insights or motivation to see beyond immediate concerns. I was incredibly lucky to have found a mentor at the beginning of my career in a coincidental manner, but had I not, I would have been well advised to seek him out in another fashion. There is some precedent for finding mentors far beyond one's level of experience:

> In Aurora Public Schools in Colorado, a group of teachers in their first three years of teaching in the district were paired with a retired mentor. . . . students taught by participating teachers had higher math and reading achievement than students of teachers with similar levels of experience who did not participate in the program. (Southern Regional Education Board, 2018, p. 3)

› **Look for an exemplar, not a master:** Strong mentors empower their mentees to achieve their goals in their own ways. They are exemplars, not masters. Masters issue commandments and expect servile obedience. Exemplars, on the other hand, show what is possible to achieve while respecting the individuality of each educator. Success is not formulaic. It doesn't have just one path. A good mentor helps you blaze your own trail and never expects you to simply walk the path he or she has paved.

› **Be the mentor you wish you'd had:** Helping others in their journeys can help you navigate changes to your own teaching career. Think about everything you wish you had known when you were a young teacher. In truth, it doesn't have to be that drastic. Think about what you wish you had known two years ago or last year. While trends come and go, certain truths and strategies never change. Mentor young teachers by helping them discover the timeless qualities of powerful teaching.

Strategy 3: Borrow, Tweak, and Share One Another's Ideas

In an era where teachers compete over test scores and are evaluated based on close adherence to strict guidelines, teachers often are not receptive to other people's ideas. They feel that they shouldn't recognize the value of a lesson, practice, or policy if they themselves did not create it, and they also hesitate to share ideas of their own that they have labored over. These habits are harmful, as they can prevent great ideas from proliferating and taking hold among an entire group of educators. The incentive to borrow, tweak, and share others' good ideas is not always obvious in an era in which the pressure to outscore other teachers is strong, test scores are often public knowledge, and schools sometimes compare and contrast everything from grade distributions to class sizes.

RIDE *the* WAVE
STRATEGY 2

Find someone you would like to have as a mentor, and write him or her a letter. Be sure to explain in the letter who you are, why you are seeking mentorship, and why you think he or she could provide the mentorship you seek. Explain the parameters of what you would want from this mentor. Do you seek just a single meeting? An ongoing email correspondence? An intensive mentorship oriented around a specific long-term goal? If you don't receive a reply within a few weeks, reach out again. If the relationship doesn't develop, try again with another potential mentor.

_____

_____

_____

_____

_____

_____

_____

_____

_____

_____

_____

_____

_____

_____

*Visit **go.SolutionTree.com/teacherefficacy** for a free reproducible version of this feature box.*

A simple change of perspective can go a long way in promoting this strategy. Instead of assuming you can't benefit from practices others have developed or fretting over others' "stealing your work"—or taking what you have created and "changing it to something you never intended it to be"—look at sharing as a symbiotic exercise of mutual admiration. Interpret sharing as complementary, not competitive. As Andy Hargreaves and Michael Fullan (2012) argue in their book *Professional Capital: Transforming Teaching in Every School*:

> Whether you are alone in your classroom or working in a team, teaching like a pro means that the confidence, competence, and critical feedback you get from your colleagues is always with you. . . . Teaching like a pro is a collective and transparent responsibility. (p. xiv)

In *Harvard Business Review*, Michael Schrage (2012), a research fellow at the MIT Sloan School's Center for Digital Business, describes a way in which he encouraged business employees to use one another's best ideas. This practice exemplifies the notion that sharing is a celebratory practice for both the workers who originate an idea and the workers who borrow it:

> The design was simple, clever and cheap: top management would recognize and reward people who demonstrated an ability to cross-functionally get real value from their colleagues and cohorts. We created two complementary yet competitive awards: "Thief of the Month"—a modest prize and high-profile internal acknowledgement for teams and small groups who "stole" an idea or innovation from another unit and successfully incorporated it into their own business; and "We Wuz Robbed"—a comparably modest prize and recognition for having one's group's best practice or process adopted by another internal group. (Schrage, 2012)

Schools can, of course, create their own version of this practice, though "Thief of the Month" and "We Wuz Robbed" are ingenious. Schrage (2012) is correct to observe that, at the end of the day:

> People don't become more collaborative or better collaborators just because you give them excellent tools for sharing any more than they cook more or prepare better meals because you give them excellent food processors and ovens. What made our little competitions work was a call for and a commitment to treating one's colleagues as value-added resources and customers for innovation and ideas. We asked people to become more intrapreneurial and open to internal offerings.

RIDE *the* WAVE
STRATEGY 3

Think about ideas you have "stolen" from your peers and things you do in your work that you think your colleagues should "steal" from you. Record the best ones, along with names of the educators who came up with the ideas, ensuring that team members receive the credit they deserve. Ask your teammates to create their own lists, and then share your responses at your next team meeting. If you hear some ideas you like, record them here, and try them in your own classroom.

Best Ideas I Have Stolen

1.

2.

3.

Ideas People Should Steal From Me

1.

2.

3.

New Ideas I Want to Steal

1.

2.

3.

*Visit **go.SolutionTree.com/teacherefficacy** for a free reproducible version of this feature box.*

Strategy 4: Show Up for Your Colleagues

Teachers take great pride in their programs, their classes, and the teams they coach. When teachers have great success in these areas, their success is not whimsical—it surely occurs because teachers demand the absolute best from their students. However, sometimes loud accolades for one teacher on staff can feel like a diminished recognition of the efforts of others on the same campus. There is a finite amount of attention and adulation to share on a school campus, only one front page of the school newspaper, only so many articles that are written in local papers or highlighted on social media platforms. This can lead to turf wars on a school campus, which are toxic, alienating, and unhelpful in an era where staff cohesion and unity are necessary bulwarks against the stress of constant change. Yet these wars are understandable. As writer and educator Jordan Catapano (n.d.) observes in "Relationship Building With Teacher Colleagues," "Often we take these relationships for granted. We focus on our students, ignore others around us, and even allow negative perceptions to infiltrate our way of thinking about others." To show up for your colleagues and not focus solely on your own efforts, consider implementing the following practices.

> **Avoid fiefdoms:** Always remember that no teacher is bigger than the school. No matter how much acclaim or how many headlines an individual teacher or program may garner, an egalitarian spirit undergirds every school staff. Each teacher is hired to carry out a specific educational mandate. Just because an individual teacher receives more attention than others does not mean that he or she has a more important task than others who work in relative anonymity. Teachers who care only about their own classes, programs, or teams, who view themselves as only coaches or program heads, are less willing to share student time. Also, they are less willing to understand how their focus undermines other laudable goals or how isolation undermines the broader educational mission of the school.

> **Embrace the educator label:** Embracing the label of educator can help avoid tension among colleagues. *Educator* is a deliberately broad term, as it denotes that one engages in the important but arduous process of educating other human beings. Why not use the title *coach*, *teacher*, or *administrator*? All these are profoundly admirable roles, but they sometimes allow members of a school community to forget that they belong to a larger team, which can cause tension. Becoming "educated" requires a battery of skills, knowledge, and personal influences. Our students learn different skills and forms of knowledge from the many voices in their lives. And coaches, teachers, and

advisers must recognize that, although they inculcate unique aptitudes and make varying demands of students, their most essential role is as team members who aim to maximize all students' capacities and possibilities.

> **Root for students in an arena other than your own:** Students and parents appreciate it when an algebra teacher shows up to a swim meet or when the football coach gives up time on a Saturday to judge rounds for the debate team. But teachers appreciate the attendance of their colleagues even more. Unfortunately, 21st century teaching often requires isolation and thanklessness of educators. The teacher next door has no notion of how many hours an AP teacher must devote to writing letters of recommendation. The AP teacher likely has no idea how much individual attention and parental outreach is required of teachers who instruct at-risk populations. Each educator has unique burdens and rewards, especially in an era as stressful and in flux as this one. Showing other educators just how much you appreciate their efforts is a simple yet meaningful way to engender a positive esprit de corps. At the end of the day, kindness is the parent of kindness. Let this be the lesson our students learn through our treatment of our colleagues.

Strategy 5: Cultivate Bottom-Up Collaboration

Educators find bottom-up collaboration—that is, when teacher communities form from an authentic desire to solve a specific problem or meet a specific goal—more enjoyable and effective than top-down collaboration, or teacher cooperation by way of administrative or district decree. Research by Mathias Krammer, Peter Rossmann, Angela Gastager, and Barbara Gasteiger-Klicpera (2018) reveals that:

> It is obvious that teachers would rather choose teammates with a similar teaching style than those that teach differently. Along these lines, similarities in the conception about teaching also make it much easier to share responsibility when working together in the same classroom. (p. 473)

Part of professional protocol requires that teachers engage in top-down collaboration to address the issues, activities, and problems that their school administration, district, or state presents. But bottom-up collaboration is also a powerful tool when confronting frequent reform. Teachers can use this ability to define which problems and projects they wish to address on their own terms and with whom they wish to collaborate

RIDE *the* WAVE
STRATEGY 4

In the middle circle of the following diagram, write down an activity, club, or group on campus you devote significant time to helping and promoting. This might even be a program of which you are the designated overseer. In the next circle out from the center, list an activity on campus you support but would like to be more involved in, and write down how you might go about becoming more involved. In the third circle, list an activity on campus you find interesting or valuable but do nothing to support. Finally, in the outer circle, list an activity on campus you know little about and have no association with, and write down how you might learn more about it. These circles signify physical and professional distance, and this exercise serves to demonstrate the power of connecting yourself to new and different parts of your school community. Not only will making these connections be rewarding, but it will also help you understand the experiences of your colleagues.

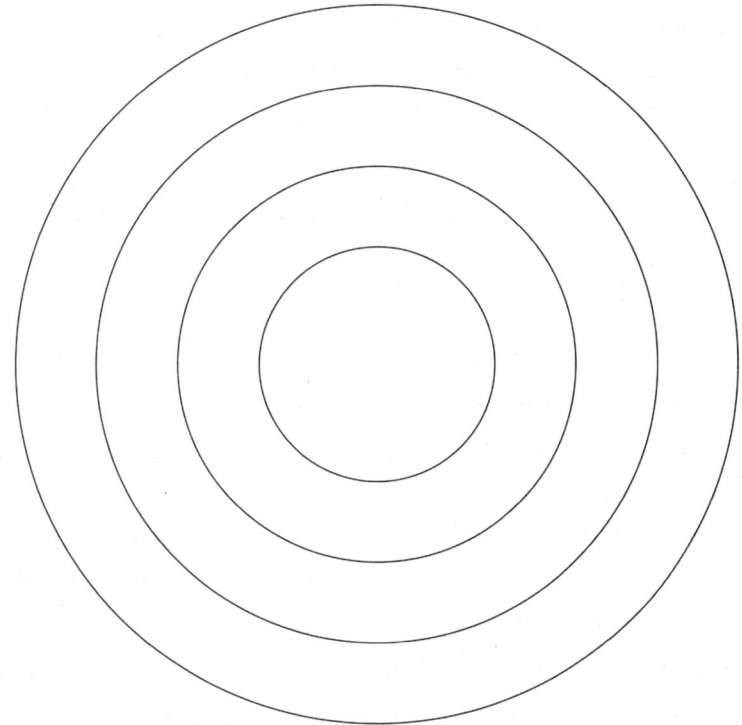

*Visit **go.SolutionTree.com/teacherefficacy** for a free reproducible version of this feature box.*

on these problems and projects. In order to cultivate bottom-up collaboration, teachers must engage in the following practices.

- **Take the initiative:** Not every problem requires a bureaucratic response. Teachers are not permanently perched in a classroom awaiting instructions on how to resolve problems bubbling up around them. As members of a school community, teachers have the power to initiate change, start innovative programs, speak out on school problems, and act creatively. Stories abound in education about normal, everyday classroom teachers who decide they are not going to wait for someone else to solve their problems. In fact, becoming a proactive educator will radically alter your vision of a teacher from one who constantly battles new waves of reform to one who sees waves as challenges to conquer and surf. The following lines of Edgar Albert Guest's poem "Sermons We See" capture the essence of this altered view's power (as cited in Stone, 1996, p. 9):

    I'd rather see a sermon than hear one any day;
    I'd rather one should walk with me than merely tell the way.

- **Find a friend:** People in all professions like to blow off steam. It is a natural, healthy way of handling the difficulty of any job. Sometimes, blowing off steam can perpetuate negativity if done to excess, but usually, it is just a harmless form of commiserating—an opportunity for teachers to voice genuine frustrations and let one another know that they are not alone in their anxieties. But there is a correct way to go about venting; you can use it as a jumping-off point to something greater and more meaningful. That is, the taking-the-initiative practice is a lot easier, and possibly more enriching, if you find a friendly colleague with whom to commiserate. Form a committee, forge a dynamic duo, or create an alliance of like-minded educators. The weight of the world becomes more manageable when you share it with others. On a basic level, teachers have supported one another for years—making copies for one another, sharing lesson plans, facilitating bathroom breaks, discussing strategies for getting the school year off to a good start, and so forth. Embodying this neighborly spirit while creatively addressing new issues that arise is an approach to bottom-up collaboration that will surely yield positive results.

- **Think local:** Many of the problems we face as educators might be national in scope, but that doesn't mean we can't have a local response to these national issues. Teachers who work to solve issues plaguing their own campuses will certainly experience a form of satisfaction and fulfillment that they would have difficulty achieving if they merely instituted changes and reforms by fiat of the district or state.

> **Have fun and involve students:** Educators can have fun with bottom-up collaboration because it is not foisted on them when they already have enough on their plates. That is why bottom-up collaboration is done, and only done, when teachers take the initiative to do so. But there is another variant of this form of collaboration: educators may also find bottom-up collaboration fun when they involve their students. In our zest to be professional and successfully manage all the expectations of the 21st century classroom, we often forget that we are surrounded by young people who are easy to smile, quick to laugh, and forever yearning to live out their natural youthfulness. In short, students are the ultimate bottom-up collaborators. Teachers who organize grassroots activities or clubs on campus or who use students to try to solve a problem at school are much more likely to find their jobs fulfilling, their students appreciative, and their colleagues eager to collaborate with them. Just as teachers who take the initiative to craft their own responses to professional stresses will find their initiative rewarding, projects inspired by student activism will mean more to students than compulsory public service. Clarizen (as cited in Team Clarizen, 2018), a collaborative work-management company, argues that "a bottom up strategy lets team members know that their views are being listened to and knowledge valued. This leads to greater loyalty and feelings of ownership among team members, as well as the advantages for the project itself."

Summary

Tension is inevitable between colleagues who work in close quarters for long periods of time. But when the stakes are high, the pressure mounts, and the list of things to accomplish grows longer as the years go on, these stressors can lead to problems among teachers on a school staff if they lack strong bonds. A taxing environment that quickly vacillates between competition, cooperation, and collaboration presents significant challenges for teachers who wish to teach within a community of supportive and like-minded professionals.

Teachers need not be lone wolves, and the profession need not be marked by conflict or jealousy. However 21st century obstacles present themselves for colleagues within a given group, the modest but significant strategies suggested in this chapter will go a

RIDE *the* WAVE
STRATEGY 5

If you could solve or address one problem on your campus, what would it be? Take the following five steps to fill out the corresponding table and create an action plan for solving that problem.

1. List who you would have to consult or enlist the help of to solve this problem. Depending on the size of the project, this might be a long list.
2. List the resources that would be necessary to develop and implement an actionable strategy for success.
3. List the obstacles that have prevented the problem from already being solved.
4. Brainstorm and list some ways to overcome those obstacles.
5. List the steps you will take to put a plan into action.

Collaborators	Resources	Obstacles	Ways to Overcome the Obstacles	Action Plan

Visit go.SolutionTree.com/teacherefficacy for a free reproducible version of this feature box.

long way in quelling teacher tensions and bolstering the spirit of a school and learning community. By following this chapter's strategies, teachers will be empowered to strengthen their relationships with one another, tackle whatever new challenges come their way, and *together* provide a more robust education for their students. In the end, this is what matters most.

PART 4

administration

While principals have a foundational role to play, they cannot bring about meaningful change by themselves. In any schoolwide change effort, there are a number of stakeholders who will be impacted, including teachers, students, family and community members, as well as school partners and district leaders and teams.

—MINNESOTA DEPARTMENT OF EDUCATION

The first administrator to ever hire me to teach changed my life forever.

Just ten weeks after graduating from college, I found myself substituting on the first day of the new school year. A former teacher of mine had to have an emergency medical procedure and asked whether I would be interested in opening the school year for her. The job would last about three weeks. I was ecstatic. The pay, the experience, the opportunity to sidestep the unpredictability of substitute teaching—I couldn't have fallen into a better position.

The students were freshmen. I didn't know who had the better excuse for first-day nerves: me, because I had to be in charge of a classroom for the first time, or them, since it was their first day of high school. But it didn't take me long to realize how much I loved the classroom.

A few days into the new school year, the principal happened to walk by my classroom and heard both a booming voice (me) and a lot of laughing (the students). I still don't know what I was saying that day as he passed by, but it made a decent impression on the principal. Later that week, he received a phone call from the district office informing him he needed to hire another teacher to reduce class sizes, and he immediately knew who he wanted to hire.

My older siblings had known this principal decades earlier when he was a chemistry teacher, and eventually, he would go on to become the superintendent of the district in which I now work. All told, he has occupied virtually every sphere in the educational universe. He has been a classroom teacher and a tennis coach. But he has also been an administrator in charge of facilities on campus, a job whose concerns are entirely different from those of typical teacher instruction. He became a vice principal in charge of curriculum and teacher schedules, which required him to manage adults, understand curricular issues and implementation, and be responsible for public engagement. He became a principal and then an assistant superintendent of the entire district. His journey is so categorically different from the career arcs of classroom teachers who remain in the classroom—and his journey exemplifies how easy it is for teachers and administrators to misunderstand one another even though they work together on the same campus almost every day.

Misunderstandings are an unfortunate side effect of working in an era characterized by waves of change and drastic reform. It takes sustained, focused effort on the part of both teachers and administrators to avoid misunderstanding and the tension it causes, so that is precisely the effort we must make. The stakes are too high for us to fail in these relationships.

Nobody likes quarreling with his or her boss. And, in education, good bosses typically yearn for a positive rapport with the teachers they mean to serve. To this end, it is important that we explore why these relationships frequently become damaged in an era of intensive change and reform. Once teachers and administrators recognize important areas of concern, they will better position themselves to avoid dissension and realize that although administrators and teachers have different tasks and mandates, their ultimate goal of providing a high-quality education to students is always the same.

CHAPTER 7

Identifying Divergent Teacher and Principal Perspectives

As much as classroom teachers often feel they are the chief stewards of a rapidly changing educational landscape, school administrators might quibble with this assessment. Teachers' seemingly never-ending list of responsibilities grows with every passing school year. However, administrators—and by this, I am referring to education professionals working at a school site who include, among others, deans, vice principals, and the principal him- or herself—would be justified to voice significant frustration on their own behalves.

Indeed, one could argue an era of constant, pervasive change thrusts school administrators into the most difficult and precarious position. The responsibilities of leading the school site are even more sobering than those of teachers. As authors Haim Shaked and Chen Schechter (2017) explain:

> School principals may be seen as mediating agents, standing at the school doorstep, between the extra-school and intra-school worlds. The principals' mediating role becomes more crucial during a time of education reform, which involves external demands on the one hand, and teachers' resistance to these demands on the other. (p. 19)

This perfectly encapsulates the cause of tension between teachers and their administrators: principals, especially in a time of reform, are "mediating agents," and this mediation is fraught with disagreement, high stakes, and, as we will see in this chapter, challenges for teachers and administrators alike. In my time as a teacher, and especially as I have worked with administrators to help deliver professional development to teachers across a wide variety of educational settings, I have realized that principals and administrators have a job that is akin to captaining an ocean liner with an especially small rudder. Principals are tasked with getting to a destination that isn't of their choosing, they have little control over the ship's design and inner architecture, they don't get to decide what to do with unruly passengers, and, most of all, they have colossal limitations in determining who serves on the crew.

If teachers are to flourish in a time of transition and reform, they must understand why they often conflict with those in administrative positions. Thus far, we have explored why constant change in the 21st century creates tension within ourselves, within our classrooms, and with our fellow teachers and, most important, what to do about it. Understanding the relationship between administrators and teachers and how to manage it, however, is a wholly different challenge beset by unique power dynamics, political ambiguity, and the potential for significant disagreement. In order to mollify whatever conflict may arise between teachers and their administration, we must first appreciate the administrator's position of powerlessness, and we must understand the spheres an administrator occupies, not only locally but also globally, outside the realm of the school site. In addition, we must realize how communication breakdowns can create turmoil in the educator ranks and ultimately lead to teacher resistance and a toxic professional environment. This chapter will provide us with these appreciations and realizations.

The Ultimate Position of Powerlessness

Teachers are frequently advised to practice empathy, and for good reason—our students sometimes endure hardships and come from backgrounds that the average person has trouble fathoming. Yet, for some reason, we rarely stretch this empathy beyond our classrooms. We should empathize with our administrators, and here's why: site administrators are situated in the ultimate position of powerlessness. Just as the average teacher sometimes has trouble fully comprehending the hardships of his or her students, so, too, is it difficult for the average teacher to appreciate the specific, often titanic, challenges faced by school administrators.

Administrators are not autonomous. They are accountable not only to their teachers and the broader public but also, more narrowly, to the superintendents of their districts and the trustees sitting on their school boards. Principals are told what direction the district wants to take, what policies need to be followed, what is being prioritized on a macro level, and what is expected to take place on a micro level. As Matt Doyle and Gerri Burton (2018) rightly comment in *Education Week*:

Identifying Divergent Teacher and Principal Perspectives

> True transformation in a school district, the kind that sticks and disrupts standard operating procedures, is fueled by school principals. It is true that the actual magic of meaningful, authentic transformation in learning happens in the interaction between the teacher, the student, and the content. . . . However, the school principal sets the conditions within which transformative practice and change happens.

"True transformation" does not happen in a vacuum, and it is not entirely localized. A principal must lay much of the groundwork for real change to occur in the classroom. Take a step back, and it quickly becomes apparent that districts, superintendents, and trustees are largely responsible for carrying out the mandates of state legislatures and the federal government. A smorgasbord of educational acronyms and initialisms—ESEA, IDEA, NCLB, and ESSA, just to name a few—act as an explicit reminder of just how many laws, mandates, and regulations districts are required to enforce, and it punctuates the enormous pressure placed on individual school principals.

However, this is just half the equation. It accounts for only the pressure principals feel from *above* them—that is, their superiors. What about the teachers they are in charge of—teachers who can exert enormous pressure on a school's administration? Principals are caught between broader government institutions and the school site they have responsibility for supervising. Figure 7.1 illustrates the principal's position in the educational ecosystem.

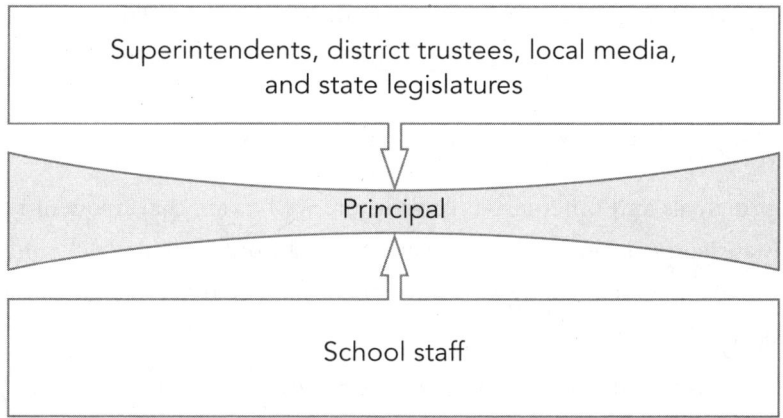

FIGURE 7.1: Principal's position in the educational ecosystem.

Teachers, especially veterans of a school staff, frequently do not hide their skepticism—or downright disdain—for new reforms. However unpleasant this pushback from teachers may be, they certainly have a good reason for it.

Professor Ewald Terhart (2013) explains the reason why teachers often push back against school principals:

> Quite frequently, they feel forced to take part in reform and development processes. This should come as no surprise; the culture and convictions of educational administrators and reformers and the culture and convictions of teachers in classrooms and staffrooms really are miles apart. Indeed, self-confident teachers may regard the approaches, ideas and recommendations of educational researchers, instructional psychologists, teacher developers, didactical coaches and so on concerning their very own field of work—classroom teaching—as being strange, clumsy or even clueless. (p. 487)

Teachers frequently direct their understandable ire toward the ultimate boss on a school campus—the principal—yet the reality is that principals oftentimes serve only as messengers, whose ability to tailor reform efforts to teacher- or site-specific needs can be severely limited. Understanding this is an important first step toward maintaining a healthy, productive relationship with the administrators on a school campus.

> ## NOTICE *the* WAVE
> What do you think would be the most difficult element of being a school principal? In what specific case have you felt especially bad for your principal because of a decision he or she had to make?

The Local and the Global

School principals and other administrators are well aware that frequent reform can sometimes ensnare teachers and administrators in an unfortunate back-and-forth for a legitimate reason: global changes to the school emanate from outside the school but must be locally implemented.

When waves of reform occur, they affect administrators' responsibilities at two levels: (1) the local and (2) the global. While administrators must tend to the well-being of their students and their staff—the local—they have additional responsibilities that are more global in nature, which the teachers on staff frequently don't notice. Global responsibilities are policies, expectations, and practices that are imposed from outside the school that require local administrators' on-site implementation and enforcement. For example, when states take up national acts and standards, such as No Child Left Behind and Race to the Top, districts then impose considerable burdens onto principals to follow the practices that were not of their own choosing. So principals must understand what needs to be achieved and how enforcement is occurring locally.

Administrators' dispensation of rules, requirements, and regulations on a site level is never easy, yet, in many cases, a good principal will shield his or her teachers from a difficult reform process in ways the teachers never fully appreciate. Principals often create more time for reform than what a district would prefer. Sometimes they break reform into incremental and thus more manageable pieces. Sometimes they give their staff a choice about implementation procedures.

When I asked one of my best friends, who went into administration after a decade of classroom teaching, how he liked administration, he made the following wry observation: "I've noticed that when something goes right, the teacher, the coach, or the adviser gets all the credit. When something goes wrong, it is always the principal's fault" (S. Anderson, personal communication, March 2018). Local, visible successes almost always place the spotlight on the professionals working directly with students. Successful implementation of global priorities, on the other hand, rarely garner much adulation. In contrast, failure in either the global or the local context always seems to be viewed as the principal's responsibility. A 21st century principal cannot exude a clueless but affable aura like Principal Belding from *Saved by the Bell* (Engel, 1989), whose catchphrase was "Hey, hey, hey, what is going on here?" A principal has to know everything that is going on, both locally and globally—and be prepared to receive little positive recognition for all the work he or she is doing.

Consider the local and global responsibilities of a school principal.

> Ensure a safe learning environment for students and staff, taking into account new worries about school violence and shootings.

> Hire teachers and fellow administrators.

> Set a schedule without stepping on too many toes.

> Shape a vision for the school.

> Create a climate where the school's vision can come to fruition.

> Nurture school leaders, and make sure responsibilities are delegated appropriately.

> Monitor all funding and expenditures on campus.

> Communicate effectively to all stakeholders, especially parents, students, teacher unions, and staff.

> Encourage professional development that is consistent with district, state, and national standards.

- Ensure staff morale is strong regardless of whatever setbacks may occur.
- Lead the process of teacher evaluation and professional development.
- Attend as many extracurricular activities as humanly possible.
- Speak at public events.
- Facilitate graduations.
- Attend award ceremonies.
- Preside over any accreditation processes.
- Be aware of policy changes to existing programs, and be mindful of new reform possibilities.
- Keep up with classroom technology needs, and monitor new developments.
- Nominate students, teachers, and coaches for honors and awards.
- Coordinate with school districts and superintendents.
- Maintain functioning facilities and a positive campus aesthetic.

At any given time, people may expect an administrator to be a leader, adviser, mentor, disciplinarian, manager, friend, visionary, public-policy savant, publicist, organizer, writer, speaker, fundraiser, accountant, human-resources specialist, or pedagogical attaché. And then there are the administrator experiences we teachers often do not see or we cannot fathom, the ones nobody wants for him- or herself—giving the eulogy at a staff member's funeral, testifying in court as part of a lawsuit, coordinating information with family members when a student dies, being publicly lambasted because of a failure at the school site, and so on. Administrators face all of this in a high-stakes, high-pressure environment dealing with students and their education, where the reputations of an institution and dozens, if not hundreds, of professionals are on the line. Such an arena can easily sow discord.

Kate Rousmaniere (2013) of the *Atlantic* distills the difficulty of being a principal in an article appropriately titled "The Principal: The Most Misunderstood Person in All of Education":

> In American public schools, the principal is the most complex and contradictory figure in the pantheon of educational leadership. The principal is both the administrative director of state educational policy and a building manager, both an advocate for school change and the protector of bureaucratic stability. Authorized to be employer, supervisor, professional figurehead, and inspirational leader, the principal's core training and identity is as a classroom teacher. A single person, in a single professional role, acts on a daily basis as the

connecting link between a large bureaucratic system and the individual daily experiences of a large number of children and adults. Most contradictory of all, the principal has always been responsible for student learning, even as the position has become increasingly disconnected from the classroom.

Phraseology like "connecting link" underscores the difficult duality of being a principal in the 21st century. No matter how thoughtful, hardworking, and kind a principal may be, managing a school site (the local) in conjunction with absorbing the broader demands of the community and policymakers (the global) places administrators on a crash course with conflict.

> # NOTICE *the* WAVE
> What items, if any, would you add to the list of principal responsibilities offered in this section (pages 109–110)? How can the principal's position as a nexus between a higher bureaucratic power and a grassroots campus life propagate conflict at times?

Ignored Voices, Hurt Feelings

Times of significant reform are perilous for staff morale. With schools changing so fast and reforms occurring in rapid succession, teachers feel perennially uneasy and unable to find their professional bearings. Unsurprisingly, teachers, especially experienced teachers, frequently resent the constancy of this unease. When a principal begins pushing a new initiative, program, or reform, the teachers on staff often ask themselves or others, "What happened to what the principal told us two years ago? Or last year? Are we supposed to just start over?"

Some resistance is inevitable, especially if a principal asks teachers to blindly get in line or embrace that which they do not understand. It is natural for teachers to feel threatened or interpret these changes as an affront to their expertise and proven abilities (Fullan, 2001). Educator Lee Ann Jung (2017) illustrates what happens when administrators decide to institute a new school policy or practice without seeking teacher input:

> As buzz generates about the policy or practice being considered, some degree of mutiny often begins to form in the school, and the shiny bubble of enthusiasm bursts. Teachers say or think things like: "It's just one more thing to do, and I don't have time." "What's wrong

with the way we do it now?" "It's only a trend. I'll wait for the pendulum to swing back the other way."

A professional chasm naturally widens between teachers and administrators when administrators make significant curriculum, pedagogy, or school culture decisions without soliciting broad feedback from the teachers on the school staff. Administrators sometimes do not inform the school staff as soon as possible or with as much detail as necessary about instituting changes. Their failure to do so makes frequent reform less palatable and the staff less receptive to it. Important questions are often ignored—questions that a number of stakeholders should be asking themselves and others. The following types of questions can get overlooked in the process.

- Is change already part of this school's culture? Does the school have a history or any record of making small but significant changes in how it operates?
- What will the skeptics probably say about the encouraged reform? Are they correct to have skepticism about it?
- Who will the proposed change affect most? Is the overarching aim of the reform worth the negative impact it might have on some stakeholders in the learning community?
- Are there any misconceptions about the proposed change that need to be addressed before moving forward?
- Does the change effort have enough flexibility that it will not disrupt the most productive and successful elements of the school?

On a basic human level, it is pleasant and affirming when faculty feel valued by the leader of the community in which they work. Even if a principal moves forward with a specific change some faculty do not agree with, merely welcoming input and feedback would help stunt hurt feelings and lessen the potential for turmoil.

NOTICE *the* WAVE

Have you ever personally felt ignored by your administrators? What was the issue, and how did it eventually get resolved? How do you respond when you feel administrators are either not seeking or not valuing your input?

Threats to a Positive and Professional Climate

When they don't face constant change, most teachers on most campuses recognize the profound difficulty of being an administrator and are quite thankful for the efforts their school leaders make. However, times of relentless reform, which put constant pressure on everyone within schools, can hamper a positive and professional campus climate, and administrators sometimes experience the brunt of this pressure in isolation.

As authors John Eller and Sheila Eller (2013) explain:

> School leaders face many challenges in implementing change. Chief among these challenges is preserving a positive climate when one or several teachers are resistant or difficult. For a school to move forward, the leader must attend to day-to-day school climate and school culture. A teacher who resists change—sometimes covertly—or who is just plain hard to work with can inject negativity into that culture. A few such teachers can derail change.

There are several types of staff members whose negative behavior and language can toxify the relationship between administration and staff. Eller and Eller (2013) pinpoint the underminer and the on-the-job retiree, though staff should also be on the lookout for the general criticizer and the island teacher.

- **The underminer:** If you're an administrator, this type of staff member "works behind the scenes to weaken your leadership by fabricating or exaggerating negative aspects about you or the change you are implementing" (Eller & Eller, 2013). The underminer often comments that the principal or other administrator in question has "been out of the classroom too long."

- **The on-the-job retiree:** This type of teacher does not challenge administrators by creating a hostile learning environment or making specific complaints about a school policy or procedure. Instead, the teacher "openly states that he or she is leaving at the end of the year and has decided to 'coast out' this time. The teacher may brag about the fact that nobody can make him or her do anything" (Eller & Eller, 2013).

- **The general criticizer:** Sometimes, teachers who are generally annoyed, overwhelmed, or burdened will make broad statements that apply to almost all administrators in the world. Statements such as "They are climbing the ladder," "All they do is stay in the office all day," and "They have forgotten the day-to-day life of a teacher" serve to simultaneously demean and denigrate the jobs that the principal and his or her fellow administrators are doing. Being a general criticizer, while certainly undermining, is more centered on giving voice to frustrations than it is about challenging any specific administrative initiative.

> **The island teacher:** This teacher does not sow division or dramatically sabotage the reform efforts of a principal. Instead, this teacher is a happy island unto him- or herself. He or she will listen politely, nod at meetings, and perhaps even give the impression of participating in the necessary collaboration. But at the end of the day, this teacher has no intention of actually participating in the school's reform effort.

Negative language, unhelpful criticism of administrators, and a general demeanor of indifference are consequences of abrupt and frequent change in teachers' work lives. And even the best principals and administrators must contend with the reality that negativity can arise in the teacher ranks. I have witnessed this myself in my two decades teaching at the same campus.

Indeed, I write these words when the only principal I have ever known, a man who has successfully and prolifically captained a large urban high school for two full decades, is only a few weeks from retirement. Teachers who have faced constant administrative turnover and strife in their careers tell me how fortunate I have been, and I do not doubt them. My principal has been an omniscient and benign presence on the campus where I teach. He has acted in the school plays; danced in the school rallies; flown in from the ceiling of a high school theater during a lively civics competition; broken up fights; and attended thousands of sporting events, extracurricular activities, and administrative meetings.

But, most significantly, he has presided over two decades of rapid, dramatic, and profound changes in educational policy and practice. And he has done so with class, vigor, and expertise. Nobody is perfect, and, of course, despite his best efforts, there was always an element of opposition to any reform movement. That said, he always upheld two values as paramount on campus. First, he insisted on moving slowly and with consensus when making significant changes to the learning environment. He was a leader who could diffuse dissension by emphasizing incrementalism and consensus. Second, and more important, before implementing a new policy, he would always ask us to consider, "Is there a significant benefit for the kids, and if so, what is it?" He never let us forget what the paramount value of any schoolwide effort must always be: the welfare of our students.

> ## NOTICE *the* WAVE
>
> How do you respond when a fellow teacher becomes negative toward the principal or other administrators? Do you personally get involved in finding a solution to the tension, or do you feel that if you are not involved in the conflict, then you should mind your own business?

Summary

The tension between teachers and administrators is largely attributable to a simple lack of understanding; these groups often don't fully understand each other's roles, capabilities, and needs. On one hand, administrators wield less power than it may seem to teachers at a school site, serving only as messengers, not architects, of policy change. And teachers are unable to realize the scope of administrators' duties, the significant work they carry out at both local and global levels. On the other hand, administrators can easily lose sight of what benefits teachers most in these complex relationships—communication and feedback, an indication that their voices are heard when it comes to decisions that affect the work they do each day.

Teacher-administrator dynamics do not have to remain tense. The following chapter will outline strategies that both administrators and their staff can use to avoid, or clean up, toxic environments and ultimately repair these relationships and maximize efficiency at the school site.

CHAPTER 8

Maintaining Staff Cohesion Through Communication

Unlike the other strategy chapters of this book, this chapter lays out recommendations that teachers *and* administrators can employ. Strategy 1 is actionable for teachers, strategy 2 is actionable for administrators, and strategies 3 and 4 are intended for both groups—though educators should familiarize themselves with *all* strategies to get a sense of what the ideal educational environment will look like if everyone is committed to his or her part. Reviewing each strategy will also give everyone a sense of what level of communication he or she may be justified in requesting if it seems communication has been cut off. Both stakeholder groups can meaningfully participate in all the strategies, tamping down tension by minding professional boundaries, welcoming and providing feedback, offering transparency, and practicing empathy, which will help create a fruitful educational environment marked by mutual support.

Strategy 1: Don't Play the Power Game

Teachers are often idealists, and idealistic teachers hope they can impart knowledge and skills that will make a difference—that will help students live better lives, professionally and personally. These teachers often seek autonomy to achieve their ideals in unique, individualized ways. As Brooklyn elementary school teacher Lily Howard Scott writes (as cited in Strauss, 2016):

> Even with a higher salary, those who would make excellent teachers will never enter the profession—or remain in it—unless schools offer them something else: the freedom to put their judgment and talents

to use to help students as best they can. This is so intuitive as to seem absurd.

Thus, there is an inherent tension between teachers who, for good reason, yearn for classroom autonomy and principals and administrators who want to change classroom practices or procedures. Many teachers fear a one-size-fits-all approach to educational reform and, frankly, tire of the false assumption that we can remedy education's ills if we simply develop a new technology, teaching trick, or curriculum. In this educational worldview, the visionaries, technocrats, and academics—many of whom rarely or never set foot in a real classroom—are empowered to dictate classroom policy and instruction in a both formulaic and highly scripted manner. As Lily Howard Scott comments (as cited in Strauss, 2016), in teachers' experience, a less mechanical approach to instruction is more natural and more effective:

> A veteran teacher recently reminded me that we bring all of ourselves to this wonderfully human complex job. Leaning into our individuality allows us to follow our instincts, which in turn enable us to connect authentically with students and tailor learning to their needs.

Playing the power game denotes the approach of a teacher who insists that his or her way is the best, or only, way. Teachers are accustomed to controlling the environments of their own classrooms and often become territorial toward outsiders proposing any type of substantive change. Getting into a turf war, however, is not productive or the least bit desirable. That is, teachers shouldn't simply follow their instincts without much consideration of directives from on high, and administrators, according to Leah Shafer (2018) of the Harvard Graduate School of Education, can't afford to lose sight of school culture—the bundle of values, principles, and behaviors specific to a school campus— "amid the push for tangible outcomes like higher test scores and graduation rates."

To avoid arguments between educators about classroom autonomy, leaders must promote school culture by creating "strong connections among every member of the school community" (Shafer, 2018). But in this process, connections can be made only if teachers, too, demonstrate they are at least receptive to change. Teachers who are interested in softening the tension between themselves and administrators would be wise to do the following.

> - **Remember who you work for:** We teachers are not sole proprietors. We are not entrepreneurs. We do not write our own standards or courses of study. We usually do not get to decide which textbooks to use. We have a mandate bestowed on us by our administrators, our districts, our states, and, in many ways, our nation. While views differ about the role a teacher plays

or ought to play in society and in students' lives, one way for us to affirm school culture and enthusiastically accept this role is to remember that we are servants of the public. The public's needs often change abruptly, which means we have to adjust. Remembering this—and even welcoming and embracing it—can help soothe potential conflict with the administrators, principals, and district officials whose job it is to respond effectively to these ever-changing needs. As Texas congressman Solomon Ortiz (2006) once said, "Teachers are our greatest public servants; they spend their lives educating our young people and shaping our Nation for tomorrow" (p. E769).

> **Accept that change will happen:** Institutions change. Sometimes they improve, and sometimes they decline. Undeniably, educational institutions of the 21st century have been the focal point for social change and improvement. Few social maladies and economic and political upheavals do not somehow find their way into school policies and expectations. David B. Cohen (2017) notes that "[the years 2000–2016] . . . have given us high-speed internet, mobile connectivity, and a variety of policy shifts—some fairly tumultuous—around testing, standards, and accountability" (p. 34), but he argues that educators must consider all proposed changes' potential to positively affect education.

Certainly, part of being an educator is walking a middle ground between advocating for changes you believe in and articulating why you think some changes should be resisted. But at the end of the day, we have to accept that there will be reform and changes to our preferred manner of doing things in the classroom and in the profession.

> **Recognize that good foot soldiers listen to their generals, even if they disagree:** We do not always have to agree with the battle plan, but we always have to maintain this hierarchy. As much as hierarchy can suppress dissent, it also creates structure within which we can make meaningful change. Without an order of command, nothing ever gets accomplished. Writer and teacher Otis Kriegel (n.d.) describes how teachers should go about listening to their principals and showing that they're receptive to change:

> > The first step is to just try what they're proposing. Even if you disagree, don't put up a fight right away. Over the years, I've been asked to try classroom techniques I disagreed with, curriculum that seemed absurd, or management techniques I was sure wouldn't work with my class. Even though I disliked these requests, I still tried them.

> **Forget the *pal* in *principal*:** As friendly as we teachers often become with our principals, it is important for us to remember that, ultimately, principals are our bosses. We need to ensure we have a professional boundary, however amicable, with administrators. No teacher ever wants to be accused of receiving favorable treatment because of a preexisting friendship. Moreover, principals and administrators must have a communal dynamic in which they can execute their jobs, which sometimes include the difficult and thankless tasks of evaluating and assessing teacher performance. As professors Sue Rieg and Joseph Marcoline (2008) observe, "Relationships must be professionally supportive, sincere, and consciously developed. After all, principals are attempting to create teams within their school, which are connected by relationships, challenge the status quo, and focus on continuous improvements" (p. 5).

Strategy 2: Welcome and Offer Feedback and Reflection

Here is what principals and administrators should provide, and what classroom teachers should want: two-way communication about what is and is not working at a school, as well as the time and space to implement needed changes.

Battelle for Kids (2011), a national nonprofit organization that provides solutions and counsel for school improvement, pinpoints five lessons that underline the necessity of both feedback and reflection in transformational educational change. While the organization largely generated this advice for school districts, it is also wise counsel for administrators on individual campuses (see Battelle for Kids, 2011, pp. 1–3). Administrators who want to build consensus, compromise, and meaningful accords of progress with their staff will find that these components are easier to come by when they employ each of the following practices.

1. **"Develop a plan that connects the work to the overall vision":** Whatever reform is being implemented, administrators should never lose sight of the campus's overall vision. There are many dots in the educational universe—comprised of everybody from the campus security officer to the state superintendent of public instruction—and connecting all of them takes a special emphasis on communication, buy-in, and the articulation of purpose. Oftentimes, reform efforts are pushed onto school sites and the administrators who run them. Implementing change in a manner that is consistent with the values, environment, and distinct persona of each campus is essential in order to avoid discord and resentment. The reform

RIDE the WAVE
STRATEGY 1

Imagine there is a new principal at your school. This principal has four questions to ask of each faculty member. How would you, as a teacher, respond to each of these questions if this new principal were to interview you? Record your answers.

Question 1: What do you expect of me?

Your answer:

Question 2: What is your preferred method of communication or resolution of an issue?

Your answer:

Question 3: What administrative practices raise your anxiety as a classroom teacher?

Your answer:

Question 4: If you were in my seat, what *one change* would you make to this school today?

Your answer:

Now the roles are reversed. What questions would you like to ask a new principal? Try to list four to five questions.

Visit go.SolutionTree.com/teacherefficacy for a free reproducible version of this feature box.

plan takes into account both the before and the after of reform efforts; administrators must understand that where they end is often contingent on a deep appreciation of where they start. No campus or staff is a blank slate on which administrators can simply graft their vision of reform.

2. **"To go fast, go alone, but to go far, go together"**: Feedback is not just any element of reform—it might be the most important one. From a principal's perspective, seeking teacher feedback can be frustrating and demanding—schools are rife with conflicting ideals, competing interests, and an almost-endless spectrum of viewpoints. However, it does not have to be the case that the teachers who disagree with a reform's direction will abstain from it. In fact, as long as the administrators responsible for implementing a reform seek teachers' input on it, most teachers will feel sufficiently respected and appreciated, even if that input isn't necessarily heeded. Teachers do not have to get their way to feel valued—but they do need to be informed and reassured that their concerns and feelings are valid. "Going together" can be arduous for a large, diverse staff; boisterous personalities and opinions can be cacophonous. But in the end, the implemented reform will be more meaningful because it will have been the collective work of all stakeholders in the school community.

3. **"Communicate, communicate, communicate"**: Administrators need to make teachers aware that whatever proposal is being made is not an indictment of the work teachers have done in the past. As the Battelle for Kids (2011) report states, "Make your message about improvement, not judgement" (p. 2). To that end, when administrators communicate requisite changes, they must alert teachers to how they are expected to act, what outcomes they are expected to gain, and what the measurements of these desirables will be. To achieve this, principals may have to communicate these ideas in a variety of ways over an extended period of time—in staff meetings, emails, workshops, individual conferences, formal and informal conversations, and so forth.

4. **"Training and support matter"**: Simply telling teachers what is expected of them does not translate into their necessarily knowing how to achieve the objective. And teachers don't always know what trainings, resources, and data are available to them. As the report comments, "Many questions arise around large-scale initiatives, and sometimes educators need assistance locating resources online, logging in to participate in online courses, or identifying the location of training" (Battelle for Kids, 2011, p. 3).

Administrators must empower teachers to live up to the mantra educators frequently offer their own students: "Be lifelong learners." Just as teachers mentor their students in what lifelong learning actually means, what it consists of, and how to truly achieve it, administrators and school districts must provide the necessary resources and opportunities if they truly expect teachers to learn new skills and enact new practices.

5. **"Celebrate and share success":** Teachers, like anybody else, like to be complimented, praised, and rewarded for a job well done. So, if administrators want their feedback to resonate—albeit somewhat indirectly—they should consider creating occasions and opportunities to highlight and celebrate classroom successes. Administrators can communicate a sense of urgency or demonstrate the importance of a practice or reform by praising those who enact it well. While most teachers of substance and conviction do not work hard strictly for headlines, accolades, and shining plaques hung on their classroom walls, this recognition still sends a powerful message to other members of the school about the type of professionalism that is expected, needed, and appreciated. Moreover, administrators should make this celebration of success as public as possible so other stakeholders can understand the value of the reform being implemented.

Strategy 3: Transform Through Transparency

Teachers are purpose people. They find purpose in their jobs and in the content they teach, and almost always, they encourage their students to find purpose in their own lives by using the education being offered to them. A logical, natural way to minimize tension between principals and teachers, then, is for principals to articulate the purpose behind any new reforms—both big and small—that they want to institute on school campuses. Teacher buy-in wholly relies on this articulation. Without transparency regarding the reason changes are being made, tension will likely develop between those pushing for changes (administration) and those who have to implement the changes on the ground (classroom teachers).

William Bridges (2009), author of the national bestseller *Managing Transitions: Making the Most of Change*, gives the following guidance, which administrators should follow:

> You need to explain the purpose behind the new beginning clearly. You may discover that people have trouble understanding the purpose because they do not have a realistic idea of where the organization really stands and what its problems are. (p. 61)

RIDE *the* WAVE
STRATEGY 2

When it comes to maximizing the chances that administrators and staff will be on the same page when implementing reform, the advice to "communicate, communicate, communicate" is about not only frequency but also variety. To this end, brainstorm the advantages and disadvantages of all the following possible forms of communication. This brainstorming is beneficial for administrators and teachers alike.

Form of Communication Between Teachers and Administrators	Advantages	Disadvantages
In-person talk		
Phone call		
Email		
Text		
Group meeting		

*Visit **go.SolutionTree.com/teacherefficacy** for a free reproducible version of this feature box.*

A principal or school leader should never cloak the reasons for change in secrecy, not even a little.

As a lifelong political science teacher, I believe it's helpful to view a principal as analogous to a president or prime minister in a democracy, not a king or autocrat in a totalitarian state. Principals, like presidents, have power and can set a firm direction, but unless they convince the people—or, in this instance, the staff—of why and how these changes need to be made, their power will be fleeting and their outcomes will be failures.

Bridges (2009) argues that this transparency can take the form of an administrator's answering the following three queries at the outset of any reform effort, which will, in turn, make the transitional period easier to traverse. The best practice is for principals and other administrators to take the initiative and address these issues without any prompting from their staff. However, there is nothing wrong if teachers feel these questions have not been sufficiently addressed and ask that their principal or administrator answer them before moving forward with any reform effort.

1. **What is the problem?** First, the administrator must explain what the problem is and why it needs to be fixed. Are test scores in a particular subject declining? Have there been breaches of school safety in the community or country? Do teachers need more time to gain professional development or master new technologies? Is there evidence that moving to a later start time will improve student outcomes and attendance? Identifying the target is an important function of a school leader. If this identification doesn't occur, then sometimes teachers might ask to collaborate with the administrator to clarify the target.

2. **How will we solve the problem, and what evidence will show our progress?** Teachers need to know that their efforts will be worth it—that they aren't simply changing for the sake of change and that they will have a way to verify when they make progress. To ensure they have harmony with their staff, principals must demonstrate that they wish to work *alongside* teachers to figure out which solutions work and which do not. As author Michael Fullan (as cited in Thiers, 2017) comments about school reform, "Research shows that the biggest factor in the effectiveness of a principal is the degree to which he or she 'participates as a learner' working with teachers to get to a solution."

3. **What would happen if no one acted to solve this problem?** Teachers take great pride in the efficacy of what they do. To ask them to alter or abolish current practices requires that they understand the ineffective consequences

of continuing on the current path. Teachers need to understand what is wrong with the status quo and what might occur if change does not happen. Drawing a vivid, perhaps dire counterfactual—that is, a picture of an alternative future in which no one has tackled or addressed the problem—is a powerful tool for getting teachers to understand the cost of inaction.

Strategy 4: Employ Empathy, Not Sympathy, and Stop Administrator Stereotypes

Students frequently confuse the words *empathy* and *sympathy*. There are certainly times when teachers can and should feel sympathy, especially in the way teachers regard their principals. Who among us wouldn't feel compassion for the plight of administrators when they are tasked with a difficult problem or are enduring an especially traumatic period in their lives or careers? Sympathy, after all, involves feeling pity or sorrow for others. This might be appropriate on occasion, but the utility of empathy is far superior.

What is truly required is *empathy*, what the *American Heritage Dictionary* (1992) defines as "identification with and understanding of another's situation, feelings, and motives" (p. 603). When teachers lack a basic understanding of or identification with the full extent of school administrators' responsibilities, they often resort to stereotyping administrators, assessing their actions are fruitless and needlessly frustrating. But administrators, too, would do well to use empathy, by demonstrating they understand the primary sources of teacher frustrations and, as a result, communicating openly. A lack of genuine empathy sours relationships that need to be strong during times of transition.

As researchers David Edgerson, William Allan Kritsonis, and David Herrington (2006) explain, "Leaders must be consummate relationship builders with diverse people and groups—especially with people different than themselves" (p. 4). Scott Van Beck (2011) conducted an extensive doctoral dissertation study of 310 public high school principals in a large Gulf Coast metropolitan area to research the causes of strong principal-teacher relationships. Specifically, his research centered on the question, "What is the most critical feature for a successful working relationship between the teacher and the principal?" (Van Beck, 2011, p. 6). In his dissertation, Van Beck (2011) pinpoints three practices that lead to a solid relationship. All three, it should be noted, involve positive behaviors and leave no room for stereotyping principals and administrators.

1. **Practice trust and respect:** Language matters. The manner in which we refer to one another matters. The regard we have for others' positions and responsibilities matters. The more teachers understand the tasks and

RIDE *the* WAVE

STRATEGY 3

In the space below, draw a circle, which will serve as the center of your word web. In the circle, write down one problem on your campus that you believe needs to be addressed with reform. In outer boxes, list different steps for solving it. You may need a number of perimeter boxes, depending on how specific your plan of action is.

responsibilities of their administrators—that is, the more they practice empathy—the less likely they will use language that denigrates or stereotypes their principals and other school officials. It is important to remember that everyone is on the same team and working toward the same goals.

2. **Communicate expectations:** Relationships flourish when people know where they stand with one another. As part of practicing empathy and bolstering mutual respect, we, as educators, must communicate what we want from one another. Teachers feel great frustration when they do not know why they are failing to fulfill the expectations of their students, their students' parents, or, in this case, their administrators. Or, to put it another way, teachers feel frustrated when they think they are fulfilling expectations only to find out they are not. Teachers already face immense expectations, so if new expectations have any ambiguity about what they are and how related behavioral changes should play out day to day, miscommunication and resentment will likely occur. A commitment to communicating expectations must be a fixture of professional behavior in an era of rapid change.

3. **Exhibit leadership:** Principals who exhibit consistent, fair, and transparent leadership are difficult to pigeonhole or stereotype as rigid or dictatorial because they always make it obvious that they view their relationship with teachers as collaborative, not adversarial. As one of the principals in Van Beck's (2011) study says about the leader-teacher relationship:

> The relationship is paramount to a well functioning school. The teachers must feel confidence in the leadership in their school. The teachers must trust the judgment and decision making of the leadership. The leadership must open the decision-making process to teachers. The leaders must trust that teachers are capable and dedicated. (p. 91)

Schools thrive and reform processes are more successful when both parties trust each other because they empathetically understand the perspective and viewpoints of the other. Teachers want principals who exhibit leadership through equity and professional treatment of the staff. Administrators are free to become the leaders they want to be if they know they are backed by a staff who have confidence in their intentions and vision.

Summary

For a teacher, a sad marker of getting older is when your students no longer recognize your cultural references. Indeed, I have had students who have never heard of Magic Johnson, Madonna, or the sitcom *Friends*. But perhaps most upsetting of all is their

RIDE *the* WAVE
STRATEGY 4

Create an interview form in which administrators and staff can ask each other questions as a basis for forming deeper professional relationships. Include the following four questions on the interview form, and be sure to add two to three of your own.

Question 1: Who or what influenced your decision to go into education as a profession?

Question 2: In your work, what is your greatest source of joy on a daily basis?

Question 3: What is something you would like to see remedied on our campus or in our building?

Question 4: What is the most surprising thing about teaching you never could have predicted?

Question 5:

Question 6:

Question 7:

Visit go.SolutionTree.com/teacherefficacy for a free reproducible version of this feature box.

ignorance of my favorite television show of all time, *The West Wing*. Unfortunately, the generation of students born during the years when *The West Wing* originally aired is more familiar with the Machiavellian characters of *House of Cards* than with the noble and patriotic efforts of the fictional president Josiah Bartlet.

The West Wing's credo (as cited in Sorkin & Glatter, 2003), "Never doubt that a small group of thoughtful, committed citizens can change the world," always resonated with me as a member of a teaching staff. While this quote was meant to describe the heroic dedication of White House staffers, it can just as accurately describe that of educators. Both teachers and administrators yearn to be part of something greater than themselves. They seek to take pride in their organization, to believe in the promise and potential of their colleagues, to understand the direction and mission of their organization, and to know that their role is essential in achieving the mission. Sadly, this form of professional exhilaration is foreign to most other members of the labor force.

Administrators and teachers can achieve this unparalleled pride, as well as positive and transformative change, through a true collaborative effort born of genuine commitment. This effort is not always easy, and the pathways to change are fraught with missteps and hurdles. Yet the way forward is crystal clear: transparent communication, mutual respect among diverse stakeholders, generous empathy between administrators and their staff when they are collectively assigned broad and difficult tasks, and, most of all, feedback and frequent, robust reflection can lessen tension between administrators and teachers and make positive, transformative change possible.

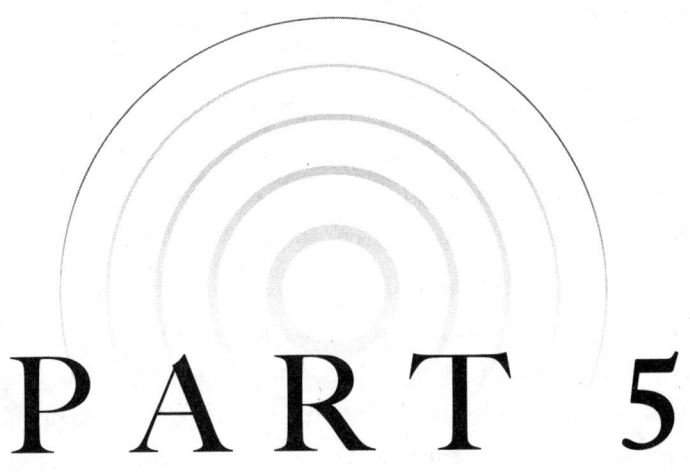

PART 5

the community

*I know no safe depository of the ultimate powers
of the society but the people themselves.*
—THOMAS JEFFERSON

It was an act of absolute serendipity.

I sat at the back of my AP government classroom listening to two students converse in an animated fashion about something I couldn't quite discern. Sadly, I could tell from their manner of speech and passionate gesticulation that they probably weren't discussing my class—or any class, for that matter. When I leaned forward, I finally realized they were talking about a football game from the previous Friday night. Their conversation quickly pivoted to Saturday college football games and the NFL games they had watched on Sunday.

I wondered, "Is there a way I could get these students to feel the same vigor and zeal for the subject I teach? Is there any way I can get them to transfer their seemingly endless enthusiasm for football to something more academic or relevant to their lives?"

It was then that I came up with the idea of a constitutional competition in which my AP government students would face one another in an event reminiscent of a single-elimination sports tournament. We would start with thirty-two students, and then sixteen would move on to the next round, until, after a total of five elimination rounds, there would be a grand champion. I decided to name the event after my high school's most famous and consequential alumnus, chief justice Earl Warren. The Earl Warren Cup gave me a chance to highlight the best and brightest students on my campus for the broader community.

The inaugural competition was held in 2006. After a few years, the competition grew to become the largest educational event in my county. During the 2016 competition, more than 1,600 citizens attended, and it ended up on the front page of the local newspaper, which also livestreamed the event so people around the world could watch.

As the competition got bigger and bigger, I arranged to have politicians and public officials record questions for my students on video. I would contact their representatives beforehand with instructions, detailing what questions they'd ask and ensuring they prefaced all questions with the mandatory "Hello, Bakersfield High School!" greeting. Public enthusiasm for the event grew over the years as the event obtained questions from two presidents (George W. Bush and Donald Trump), two justices of the Supreme Court (Elena Kagan and Anthony Kennedy), three Speakers of the House of Representatives (Nancy Pelosi, Paul Ryan, and John Boehner), two California governors (Jerry Brown and Arnold Schwarzenegger), Bill Gates, Elon Musk, Tony Blair, and numerous national media and Hollywood personalities. While the national celebrities and leaders were who drew the crowds, it was the students' display of history, civics, and current-events knowledge that most impressed the community.

Creating and holding this event taught me a powerful lesson: if you create a platform on which students can shine, the community will respond favorably. Sadly, too often, the news surrounding U.S. education is decidedly negative. But that doesn't mean the relationship between educators and the communities they serve can't improve. It can.

Teachers and the communities they serve can repair the relationship that has been damaged in a time of turbulence, tension, and far-reaching frustration if they explore why they mutually misunderstand each other. However, this meaningful engagement and informed dialogue between teachers and communities will not happen spontaneously. Teachers from all backgrounds have substantive steps they can take to both lessen communal tensions and usher in an era in which they see the public as not merely a patron but a partner in educating the community's children, so that all parties can conquer the waves of change together.

Note: while many of the educational trends discussed in this book are not U.S.-specific phenomena, the focus of this section will admittedly be on the U.S. system of education. This focus is the consequence of two factors: (1) my firsthand experiences are firmly anchored in the world of U.S. education, and (2) all communities and countries are going to have unique strengths and qualities that they can showcase, as well as unique education-related policies that they can work on. While a country may see a distinct rapport between its schools and individual communities, all readers will still benefit from reviewing the strategies offered in chapter 10 (page 143), which can further strengthen community-school relationships regardless of their current dynamics.

CHAPTER 9

Viewing Education From a Distance

Americans are educational romantics—and for good reason. They understand that virtually every value or outcome that Americans hold dear requires some sort of cultivation in the classroom. These values and outcomes include professional success; democratic self-government; critical-thinking skills; organizational ability; a sprawling battery of communication skills, including writing and speaking; and basic knowledge of important literary, historical, and scientific facts. If a pollster asked a dozen students, parents, and educators about the broader purpose of education, there is a decent chance the pollster would receive a dozen different answers. Yet there is a common link among all the answers: education is the key to a successful future, no matter how one defines success.

As much as U.S. society leans on schools to renew its institutions and cultivate its citizens' potential, it also grows frustrated with these schools when problems appear. This creates an odd dynamic: the broader U.S. public simultaneously and reflexively views educational institutions as both the culprit and the panacea—and it does so from a distance, from which it's unable to appreciate the more granular aspects of education and student achievement. Indeed, it is a colossal undertaking to explain the extent to which this conflicting duality affects U.S. schools and educators, many of whom feel positively Atlas-like because of the scope of the expectations now placed on them.

While all the various educational relationships that this book covers are vital, the broader communal dynamic explored in these final chapters is arguably the most critical. This communal dynamic might be abstract, in that the term *community* can include anything from a neighborhood to an entire country, yet it is of paramount importance, as education bolsters both the highest collective hopes of the country and the individual dreams of its young people.

In this chapter, we will explore why society's impressions of individual schools and individual teachers are generally positive while its opinions of U.S. education as a whole are generally negative, and we will look at the problems this chasm creates for 21st century educators. We'll do this by considering how teachers are absorbing the weight of the world as the public devalues their profession, how the public witnesses only schools' shortcomings, and how a single variable seems to drive the myth of systemic educational failure.

The Weight of the World

On September 17, 2018, *USA Today* did something extraordinary. It sent teams of journalists around the United States to shadow fifteen individual teachers for a school day (Hampson, 2019). This project came about because in the spring of 2017, teachers in six states went on strike in protest of grievances they had about the state of the teaching profession, among them "compensation and school spending" (Hampson, 2019). Those who operate outside the profession seemed surprised by this visible dissent from the corps of American teachers. As the article notes, those of the general public tend to think they know educators, as they were once students in the classroom and interacted with teachers each day. "But the suddenness and vehemence" of the widespread protests indicate the public does not in fact appreciate teachers' "pressures and frustrations" (Hampson, 2019).

This articulates the fact that the gulf between teachers and the communities they serve is qualitatively different from the conflicts teachers experience in themselves, in their classrooms, with fellow teachers, and even with administrators. Students, teachers, and principals live their lives in a common professional space. But the broader public does not share this relationship with education or work in a common professional space with teachers. The public does not always understand that teachers feel they are absorbing the weight of the world in a way that those of other professions do not experience. Though the *USA Today* journalistic teams followed only fifteen American teachers, the conclusions they draw are powerful and truly reflective of teacher experiences across the country:

> Teachers are worried about more than money. They feel misunderstood, unheard and, above all, disrespected.
> That disrespect comes from many sources: parents who are uninvolved or too involved; government mandates that dictate how, and

to what measures, teachers must teach; state school budgets that have never recovered from Great Recession cuts, leading to inadequately prepared teachers and inadequately supplied classrooms. (Hampson, 2019)

Poll after poll from between 2008 and 2015 reveals that teachers have taken a decidedly pessimistic view of their profession and its future. The *Washington Post* argues that "the real reasons behind the U.S. teacher shortage" and the exodus of teachers from the profession have less to do with teacher salaries and more to do with "a combination of under-resourced schools, the loss of job protections, unfair teacher evaluation methods, an increase in the amount of mandated standardized testing and the loss of professional autonomy" (Strauss, 2015). The article cites a dizzying array of teacher opinion polls, none of which suggests that teachers feel supported by leaders or respected by the public. According to the opinion polls, teacher satisfaction declined 23 percent from 2008 to 2013, the percentage of teachers getting a teaching license fell by more than 50 percent from 2009–2010 to 2013–2014, and, perhaps most disturbing of all, by "nearly a 5 to 1 margin, respondents said that they would not recommend teaching as a profession" (Strauss, 2015). As Paul Toner, former president of the Massachusetts Teachers Association, argues (as cited in Ferguson, 2018):

> The big issue facing the profession is just generally making it a career that people want to enter and stay in for at least a reasonable period of time, like 10 or more years. It is about sustainability of the profession. It is at times a very stressful job depending on your work environment.

I am the child of two teachers and the sibling of teachers, and I can honestly say that my best friends in the world are teachers. So, of all these statistics, polls, and studies, the one I find most demoralizing is the 2018 Phi Delta Kappan (PDK) public opinion poll, in which members of the public were asked about teaching as a career path. For the first time ever, "more than half of respondents (54%) said they would not like a child of their own to make a career out of teaching in the public schools" (Ferguson, 2018). There are two possible conclusions that we can reach from this distressing discovery, neither of which is good, and each of which reveals the colossal stress teachers now experience. First, the public does not hold teaching in particularly high esteem, and thus, parents want their children to find a more laudable profession. Second, the public is aware, though not *fully* aware, that teaching has become an arduous profession, and parents would rather their children avoid it altogether.

> ### NOTICE *the* WAVE
> Do you believe the profession has lost prestige over the course of time? If so, which misunderstandings about education among the broader public do you think have affected its prestige? Would you want your children to go into education in some capacity? Why or why not?

High-Profile Shortcomings and Underreported Strengths

Pundits, prognosticators, and commentators of all stripes and political backgrounds take it for granted that U.S. education is failing and that something new or innovative must be done to overhaul it. Comparisons to education in other countries, cherry-picked statistics, and sensationalized headlines highlighting the shortcomings of our schools lend credence to the narrative that U.S. education is in decay and even in the desperate throes of malfeasance.

To be sure, educational institutions across America have authentic failures. We cannot and should not deny this. High school dropout rates are too high. Funding mechanisms are outdated, and they disproportionately disadvantage poor and minority students. The best teachers have a profound disincentive to teach the most destitute students. Literacy and higher-order-thinking skills are in decline. Knowledge of the United States' history and political institutions is so poor—not just among students but the public writ large—it is its own separate civic crisis in the making. These shortcomings often bleed into the wider adult population, creating a loop of dysfunction in which poorly educated adults do not know how to perpetuate the values, institutions, and behaviors that are necessary for a free and democratic society to flourish. Cycles of failure are easy to blame on schools, educational institutions, and the like. This habit of targeting and casting culpability onto schools for broader social dysfunction and disappointment is one of the central reasons why schools have become epicenters of constant reform. Schools are viewed by the broader public as breeding grounds for whatever it is mass society wants to encourage or perpetuate. The more we ask schools to do, however, the more there is the potential to blame the very institutions we cast as bases of reform.

The distance between the scores of the wealthy and the scores of the poor is stubbornly wide. Teacher morale on a national level is glum, and even that is perhaps putting it generously. Teachers are leaving the profession in droves, and some experience a form of public animosity they never expected. For example, according to lecturers Paulina Billett, Edgar Burns, and Rochelle Fogelgarn (2019), 80 percent of Australian teachers have experienced some form of harassment or bullying from parents or students. These teachers, says professor Peta Stapleton (2019), find themselves to be "more depressed and anxious than the average Australian."

But much of the tension between educators and the communities they serve is caused by a concerted effort to focus solely on the profession's failures, never on the profession's successes, in the media. A famous axiom in media circles says that it's not the media's job to report on the planes that land. Fair enough—but much of what the U.S. public hears of education leads people to conclude that all schools and teachers are crashing, or failing in their attempts to provide a high-quality education to students, no matter that the plane is overpopulated, the engines are outdated, and the services expected on a flight exceed what its attendants were trained for.

In *Education Week*, teacher trainer Pat Quinn (as cited in Baeder, 2012) notes an argument could certainly be made that our "system of education that has been created for students in kindergarten through high school is the best educational system in the world. No exceptions. No disclaimers." He supports this argument by reminding readers that U.S. teachers and schools have unique challenges but also, at the same time, try to achieve more than the teachers and schools of virtually any other country in the world.

American schools are guided by an egalitarian commitment to provide education to all students that would make the likes of Horace Mann proud. Education in America is not the domain of only the privileged or the powerful. Nothing is more fundamental to U.S. values than ensuring every child receives the opportunity to make the most of his or her individual talents and opportunities. This is the spirit of the Fourteenth Amendment, the hope of *Brown v. Board of Education*, and the expectations of countless state constitutions.

This commitment to include all students extends to the standardized testing regimen we have implemented in the United States. Unlike in other countries, where only the best students are tested, in the United States, all students are tested, regardless of background or class, which play such a pivotal and predictive role in academic measurements. Indeed, as Gary Sands (2017) of *Forbes* reports:

> What this means in practice is the ability of some education administrators [to choose] their top-performing students from smaller samples in cities or city-states such as Chinese Taipei, Macao, Hong Kong and Singapore. While most of the other results came from a sample of scores around nations, some countries such as Argentina and China were allowed to take their sample from their most educated cities or regions.

This difference in testing regimens gives the mistaken impression that the United States is lagging far behind other industrialized powers.

Interestingly, I have noticed over the years that exchange students usually find American teachers more personable than teachers from their home countries. This facet of education would never come through in a standardized-exam score. I have always been curious about how U.S. schools and classroom environments differ from what these students are used to back home. I have had bright—and in some cases brilliant—students from countries such as Germany, Sweden, and Italy. Of course, these students' answers are only anecdotal, but they always mention appreciating that American teachers generally attempt to create a positive and affirming relationship with their students. Or, as one of my German exchange students humorously remarked, "You talk about your wife and kids and try to make us laugh. That would never happen back home."

In addition to providing broad access to education and testing, the United States puts significant resources and time into its students most at risk and vulnerable. Its commitment to students with special needs is unmatched. As Quinn (as cited in Baeder, 2012) notes, "The United States has developed a system of educating special education students that is vast and complex." And finally, the breadth and diversity of the subjects taught and programs offered on U.S. campuses are unsurpassed the world over. Unlike hierarchical European systems of schooling or rigid Asian programs that have little variance in either curriculum or pedagogy, the United States' rich, varying panorama of subjects and programs caters to individual students' abilities, interests, and circumstances. Everything from the traditional arts and athletic programs to a new emphasis on STEM education is present in virtually all schools in the United States. Not many countries can say this.

And not many Americans are aware of just how much the country's schools do for young Americans, especially in the area of extracurricular activities and sports. As Amanda Ripley (2013b), author of the bestseller *The Smartest Kids in the World* (Ripley, 2013a), notes in the *Atlantic*, "In countries . . . like Finland and Germany, many kids play club sports in their local towns—outside of school. Most schools do not staff, manage, transport, [or] insure" such teams. Not only is the United States unique in the number of activities schools facilitate beyond classroom instruction, but there appears to be a significant payoff for schools ensuring their availability. Researchers Margo Gardner, Jodie Roth, and Jeanne Brooks-Gunn (2008) report, after examining the results of a longitudinal study, that "youths who participated in organized activities for 2 years demonstrated more favorable educational and civic outcomes in young adulthood than those who participated for 1 year" (p. 814).

> # NOTICE *the* WAVE
> What types of programs and services provided on campus would come as a surprise to the average citizen who has little interaction with schools? Do you think there is an argument for schools to do less? Why or why not?

The Myth of Systemic Educational Failure

When studying the U.S. Congress, my political science students are often baffled by two seemingly contradictory pieces of information. First, when we look at the approval ratings of Congress as an institution, the percentage rates are generally so low, usually hovering somewhere in the teens, that students mistakenly assume most members of Congress lose their reelection bids (Gallup, n.d.b). But then, I teach them that most Congress members get reelected in landslide contests—generally, more than 90 percent of members of the House of Representatives win reelection, sometimes without breaking much of a political sweat (OpenSecrets, n.d.). How can we reconcile these two disparate pieces of information? Simply put, Americans distrust Congress but have a high regard for their individual congressperson. They believe that if the institution is broken, unresponsive, or hyperpartisan, it isn't because of *their* representative; it must be the *other* representatives.

Americans' views of the U.S. educational system reflect virtually the exact same phenomenon. For example, in the last week of the school year, I ask my graduating seniors to reflect for a minute on the last thirteen years of their lives and to assign letter grades to their overall K–12 educational experience. And they rarely give anything other than an A or a B. Their parents would certainly agree; in the *Atlantic*, Jack Schneider (2017) writes that when parents are asked to rate their own children's educational experiences, they grade them quite highly, with almost 70 percent giving As and Bs. Yet when asked to reflect on the national level of educational excellence, almost 70 percent assign a grade of C or D (Schneider, 2017). While their own experiences are largely positive, their general impression is decidedly negative. And this negativity from the U.S. public has profound ramifications for the career arc of American teachers.

As Schneider (2017) eloquently explains:

> Consider the impact on policy. If the nation's schools are generally doing well, it doesn't make sense to disrupt them. But if they are in a state of decline, disruption takes on an entirely new meaning.

Seizing on the presumed failures of the education system, reform advocates have pushed hard for contentious policies—expansion of charter schools, for instance, or the use of value-added measures of teacher effectiveness—that might have less traction in a more positive policy climate.

Schneider (2017) calls this divide between the U.S. electorate's personal experiences of schools and its generalized impressions of them a "perception gap" of U.S. education. He says the pessimism is fueled by a number of factors, including the "rise of a national politics of education" that includes everything from Sputnik in 1957 to more modern attempts, such as the Every Student Succeeds Act of 2015 (Schneider, 2017). But at their core, public frustrations are driven by now widely available data—primarily standardized-test scores—that reveal much more about a student's income level or neighborhood status than they do about the quality of the student's teachers.

In a 2018 study titled *The (Mis)measure of Schools: How Data Affect Stakeholder Knowledge and Perceptions of Quality,* Jack Schneider, Rebecca Jacobsen, Rachel S. White, and Hunter Gehlbach (2018) found that "when users of a more holistic and comprehensive data system evaluated unfamiliar schools, they not only valued the information more highly but also expressed more confidence in the quality of the schools" (p. 1). In other words, the data that communities have broadly available about their schools—which disproportionately rely on a single variable, standardized-test scores—are not particularly accurate or revealing regarding their schools' quality. When communities rely solely on these data, they underestimate their schools' quality. But when people hear, for example, about factors such as a school's excellent drama program, its emphasis on student interventions, or its commitment to lowering suspension and expulsion rates, the percentage of approval significantly increases.

Moreover, Schneider et al. (2018) emphasize in the conclusion of their study that communities' overreliance on test scores has another subtle but equally powerful consequence. Simplified data that do not look at other factors may well "exacerbate segregation patterns by steering well-resourced and quality-conscious parents away from perfectly good schools, and in doing so, they may enact a self-fulfilling prophecy by concentrating inequality" (Schneider et al., 2018, p. 19). Indeed, some of the best teaching in America is done on campuses that do not necessarily have the best standardized-test scores. When citizens disaggregate and look at everything that goes into the educational process, they have a much more positive assessment of U.S. education than if they reflexively look at a single measure.

> ## NOTICE *the* WAVE
> Can you recall a time when your school had to respond to community members' criticism (for example, of its standardized-test scores)? If so, how did your school react? Was the impulse to assure the public that the school would work to improve in the area that received negative attention, or did the school attempt to counter negative assessments with alternative data?

Summary

It is natural for teachers to feel underappreciated, misunderstood, and woefully underresourced by the broader public. As teachers work through their never-ending to-do list (see chapter 3, page 39) in an effort to provide high-quality education to all students, the public sees a system characterized by flaws. As I have noted in this chapter, much of the tension between teachers and the public is fueled by a fundamental misunderstanding about the diverse services that schools and teachers provide and the public's narrow measurements and generalizations of school and teacher quality.

In the next chapter, we'll learn ways to correct the U.S. public's tunnel vision by putting teachers and students in direct contact with citizens and making a broad, accurate representation of education success fully visible.

CHAPTER 10

Connecting Citizens and Schools

By using the following three strategies, you'll give the citizens of your community the opportunity to peer into and even become part of the most intimate, essential space within education, one that many people have completely lost sight of—the classroom. Once the public is made aware of your school's and students' triumphs; interacts directly with current students inside and outside the classroom; and acknowledges the school's role in sustaining a democratic society of civil, well-rounded individuals, it will have no choice but to abandon its narrow criteria for what makes a U.S. school special and successful.

Strategy 1: Highlight Successes

Much of the negativity that the public directs toward schools and educators originates from a lack of knowledge. The broader public does not know of the heroic efforts of so many educators in its own community. People lack awareness of the pressures that are present in classrooms or how much innovation teachers develop to combat these pressures. They are not cognizant of the high hurdles placed in front of teachers daily and how often teachers conquer these hurdles with dignity, grace, and unparalleled professionalism. To address this ignorance, teachers should get into the habit of highlighting their own successes. While modesty, restraint, and quiet excellence are certainly virtues, advocating for the good work of one's profession also has its benefits. To this end, try these methods of highlighting successes in your classroom and at your school.

> **Become a social media ninja:** This doesn't necessarily come easy to those of us who have been in the profession for a long time. And the truth is

that learning how to navigate, use, and be prolific on different social media platforms can be a little scary, especially for teachers who are used to operating in relative obscurity. The language of hashtags, retweets, and the like might seem as foreign a language as ancient Greek. For better or for worse, however, the world gets much of its news from these platforms in the 21st century. While Twitter, Instagram, and Facebook might seem to be the domain of students, schools can easily highlight many worthy classroom activities and achievements on such forums.

Oftentimes, school districts lead the charge in using social media as a medium of promotion. And, as writer Shawna De La Rosa (2018) points out in an article exploring the efforts of Collier County Public Schools in Florida, teachers who follow their districts' lead generally find the experience to be positive. Social media helps connect parents to the classroom, assists teachers in joining together students from around the world, and can even tie authors and public figures to individual classroom activities. However, teachers should remember that each platform has its own strengths and weaknesses (De La Rosa, 2018)—

- "Twitter, though not as popular with parents, seems to be the best way to link students to faraway classrooms."
- "Educators can share big and small wins on Facebook because most parents use the social network."
- "Instagram posts are more about the photo than the text—the image should tell a story on its own, and include a brief explanation."

Of course, you should always be aware of drawbacks (for example, sometimes people post hurtful comments on social media posts) and ensure professional language, content, and practices at all times. Putting information into the public arena will sometimes result in trolling or criticism, but this is typical of social media posts—no matter how neutral or noble the message—and a relatively small cost for promoting worthwhile efforts in the classroom.

› **Be your own PR agent:** If you want the public to hear your classroom successes, sometimes you must pick up the megaphone yourself. Granted, this might take you out of your safety zone as an educator, either because you aren't familiar with the social media world or because you're not accustomed to activities associated with promotion. It might also make you feel as though you're artificially drawing praise or fishing for compliments from the public. But as long as you focus on the students' successes and efforts, this will likely paint schools and teachers in a more positive light. As writer Betsy Potash (2018) advises:

> Sometimes the best way to alert the media about the great things happening at your school is to be the media. Write a positive letter to the editor, a column for the local paper, or a piece for a magazine. Even blogs or certain websites are good outlets.

> **Nominate fellow teachers for recognition:** Putting a bright spotlight on exemplars of the profession is a significant way you can improve the public's perception of teachers. While individual schools usually have their own annual awards or honors, these recognitions rarely get much notice beyond a localized school site. Fortunately, multiple national, and even global, programs serve to highlight the extraordinary achievements of everyday classroom teachers. In addition to the most famous National Teacher of the Year Program, operated by the Council of Chief State School Officers (CCSSO) since 1952, there are numerous other prominent, prestigious programs, such as the Milken Educator Awards (www.milkeneducatorawards.org), the NEA Foundation Awards for Teaching Excellence (www.neafoundation.org/for-educators), the Carlston Family Foundation (www.carlstonfamilyfoundation.com/nominate), and the Pearson National Teaching Awards (www.teachingawards.com). There is even a National Teachers Hall of Fame in Emporia, Kansas (www.nthf.org), and a Global Teacher Prize that comes with a $1 million reward (www.globalteacherprize.org). Even if local teachers do not win these awards, your simply nominating them helps underscore the educational successes in your community.

> **Get students involved in their own promotion:** Highlight classroom successes by creating assignments and activities that have a public or communal element to them. This can take virtually any form. For example, if students are preparing a presentation, open up the presentation to the public. Make it a nighttime presentation, and hold it in an auditorium instead of in a classroom. Find a way to stream the event live on Facebook or YouTube. If students have to complete a writing assignment, design an assignment that could be published in the local or school paper, and make sure students submit their work to the publication. Allow and encourage students to do what they do best: post their work and activities on social media in a way that brings notice or acclaim to their efforts and excellence. Maybe a post will even go viral and the wider community can take note of student achievement.

RIDE *the* WAVE
STRATEGY 1

Create three hashtags that are appropriate for promoting your classroom activities.

1.

2.

3.

List three people in your community you should connect with to promote site activities.

1.

2.

3.

List three colleagues to honor, and give a brief summary of why each is worthy of the honor.

1.

2.

3.

List any other actions that will allow you to promote your students' and your classroom's successes for the current school year or future school years.

_____

_____

_____

_____

Visit *go.SolutionTree.com/teacherefficacy* for a free reproducible version of this feature box.

Strategy 2: Look in the Rearview Mirror

It is natural for citizens, as they age, to forget the vitality, texture, and general atmosphere of a school. Any teacher married to a person not involved in education can testify to this!

Most citizens' direct involvement in the schooling experience is limited to their own education—chiefly, what it was like when they sat in a classroom, watching a teacher teach. Involving the broader public in the educational process would give these citizens a fresh and more positive perspective on the educational system. It would show community members not only what it is like for students to attend school today but also what it is like for teachers to serve a diverse audience of students. To this end, the following teacher practices invite community members to look in the rearview mirror of life, or remember their own schooling experiences, in such a way that it helps students and bolsters communal appreciation for the teaching profession.

> **Use community members in lessons:** Public officials certainly enjoy being asked to come to classes and participate in student programs—and it's part of their job—so mayors, city council members, district trustees, and the like make terrific speakers for students. A less conventional but equally powerful engagement practice is to invite members of the public who possess expertise in a subject being taught. Invite an accountant to a mathematics class. Invite a business owner to an economics course. Bring in local published writers to discuss their craft with students at any age level. The possibilities are endless.
>
> In addition to repairing the fracture between schools and communities, this practice is also a practical instructional technique. Students are forever pursuing the *why* behind any subject or lesson, asking teachers questions such as, "Why do I need to know mathematics?" "Why do I need to be able to communicate effectively?" and "What benefit is there to knowing the history of the country or even the planet?" Teachers can find it tricky or awkward to provide justification in this context. So who better to answer these needling questions than the professionals who use this foundational information, and who themselves learned this information in school?
>
> These community members can take part in lessons in any number of ways, from giving a traditional lecture to leading a workshop or facilitating a Socratic seminar. As digital strategist Kara Wyman (2017) points out, providing this type of student-community connection will "[give students] real-world experiences and [help] you maximize available resources." This

will show students that inspiring and fulfilling careers don't usually happen by accident; there is a natural pathway, for example, from algebra and geometry to the field of aerospace, or from political science and history to the field of law. But beyond all of this, you'll give community members a role—the opportunity to be among students and to understand their experiences but also to appreciate the position of the educator.

> **Bring in former students:** Involving former students in the classroom benefits current students because it allows them to build a strong connection with those who recently confronted similar problems. These former students can run the gamut from recently graduated to newly hired in the workplace and can even include individuals a decade or more removed from graduation. Finding people who share a fidelity to a certain school builds a connection and genuine credit in the eyes of students. After all, former students can always claim a common launchpad with students sitting in the classroom. And current students meeting with alumni can learn about pathways to careers and experiences that they are only dreaming of at this point in their lives. Jessica Lander (2016), a high school teacher and 2015 graduate of the Harvard Graduate School of Education, tells the following story about using former students as teacher apprentices in her current classes:

> > Two of my recently graduated high school seniors, now college freshmen, arrive at my classroom at 7:15 a.m. every Friday morning. As I unlock my door, they ask, "So what are we teaching today?"

> > The two former students are incredible—they stay all day, acting as teachers and mentors in my U.S. and World History classes. Many college freshmen might prefer to sleep in on days they don't have classes. Not these two. During a lesson exploring two speeches by President Woodrow Wilson, they circulate, helping students define words, asking others to push their thinking further, answering questions while I'm working with another student. Another day, during a vocab quiz, they watch their former peers, eagle-eyed, making quiet and quick reminders to students to keep their focus on their papers.

> While Lander's example centers on recently graduated students and she uses them in a rather proactive fashion—all-day presence, circulating around the room—it is important to note that the utility of using a former student is strong even if his or her appearance constitutes a short onetime event. Former students can make a significant impression by showing current

students that they are taking time out of their normal professional lives to assist them, and perhaps explaining or demonstrating what awaits students on the horizon of adulthood. The truth is that oftentimes students have been listening to the same voices of their teachers and parents for so long that a fresh voice can break through in a way that everyday voices cannot. Admitting and playing to this is no defeat.

One of my proudest achievements as a teacher is the number of positive friendships I sustain with former students. Of course, most of these students still call me Mr. Adams, and no matter how old or accomplished they become, each will always primarily be a student to me. All of them seem to look back fondly on their time in my class and in school in general, no matter how many years have passed. Because they understand that I was there for them as a teacher, most former students are happy to help if they are asked to return the favor. I have had dozens of students return to the classroom where I once taught them, so that they may speak to my current students about a variety of topics and in a number of forums. So if you maintain these relationships and call on these former students from time to time to fill specific roles in the classroom, chances are they'll be thrilled to participate—and you will not only give them a rarified educational opportunity but also make a considerable contribution to the effort to improve relations between the public and schools.

> **Go out into the community:** While bringing community members and former students into the classroom is effective, it can be equally useful to send students out into the broader community. You have numerous ways in which you can encourage students to leave the conventional classroom setting in favor of more active learning and civic engagement. Visit local libraries and museums as a class. Link lesson plans with local organizations that advance different social causes, or find incentives for students to reach out to local businesses to obtain information related to a class assignment. Have students engage in community activities after school for class credit, either individually or as a group. Promote volunteerism for causes the students believe in.

When students go out into the community, it has the benefit of allowing teachers to reconfigure what the learning process actually looks like so students see that not all learning has to take place within a classroom or at a school site. Students know their learning is now linked to the real world. Simultaneously, this community engagement creates a productive and inclusive context within which students and community members interact. Any avenue that fosters a productive dialogue and creates positive platforms for community engagement is likely to substantially improve relations between schools and different stakeholders within the broader community.

As mentor Brendan O'Keefe (2011) observes:

> Much of what we learn as children and adults happens outside the classroom through real world experiences from our peers, mentors or on the job.
>
> How might we connect today's core curriculum with the real world? That is an important question that is in urgent need of answers. Kids today are asking far too often for relevance in what they are learning.

Encouraging a symbiotic partnership of schools and community members is the solution to the conundrum O'Keefe identifies. It answers student questions about curricular relevance as community members can anecdotally explain the linkage between classroom learning and real-world productivity. But let us not forget that every adult was once a student and perhaps needs only for schools to facilitate the interactions that will place them alongside students and teachers once more—so that they may reflect on their own positive educational experiences, humanize the learning environment, and feel both hopeful about and invested in the future success of those on campus.

Strategy 3: Demonstrate Democracy

Teachers can also meaningfully ease tensions between communities and the educational institutions that serve them by embodying and practicing the behaviors that a democratic society needs in order to flourish. Indeed, a powerful and convincing argument could be made that U.S. educational institutions are no different from other civic institutions that have also witnessed profound decreases in public trust.

From 1973 to 2018, Gallup (n.d.a) measured the extent to which Americans had a "great deal" or "quite a lot" of confidence in a broad collection of institutions that govern different elements of public and private life. The results of this study are alarming if not catastrophic. Confidence in church or organized religion dropped by 27 percent, and confidence in Congress dropped by 31 percent in those forty-five years. In the same time span, confidence in newspapers went down by 16 percent, confidence in the presidency went down by 15 percent (and 1973 was in the middle of the Watergate scandal!), and confidence in the medical system precipitately declined by 44 percent (Gallup, n.d.a). Viewed in this context, a 29 percent loss of public trust in

RIDE *the* WAVE
STRATEGY 2

Plan a community event in which a panel of former students and community members will gather to conduct a forum on a topic that is relevant to one of your classes. You can use the template that follows to plan this event, contact the panel members, and confirm their participation.

Community Event Planning Template		
Topic:		
Date and location of event:		
Panel Member	**Contact Information**	**Confirmation of Attendance** (Check this box when the panel member has confirmed.)
Former student 1:		
Former student 2:		
Community member 1:		
Community member 2:		

Visit **go.SolutionTree.com/teacherefficacy** *for a free reproducible version of this feature box.*

public schools is certainly upsetting, but it can be understood as part of an era of deep cynicism about U.S. civic life.

While the failure of U.S. schools has been unjustly exaggerated and overreported, schools and teachers can play a pivotal role in repairing the tattered 21st century body politic if they model the following three behaviors in their communities and their classrooms. Professor Joel Westheimer (2017) presents these behaviors in *Educational Leadership*:

> Public schooling in America has always been implicated in nurturing civic capacities and habits consistent with democratic life. Educating citizens requires that schools take seriously the need to nurture two essential elements unique to democratic life: asking challenging questions and considering varied perspectives. Schools can achieve these goals by focusing on three practices: teaching students how to ask questions; exposing students to multiple perspectives; and rooting instruction in local contexts.

1. **Ask the difficult questions:** Discourse and debate are hallmarks of a democratic culture. The capacity to ask difficult questions, openly challenge conventional thinking, and offer unorthodox perspectives is an essential value of democratic life. It has been essential from the ecclesia of ancient Athens to the state ratification conventions of the late 1780s, to 21st century disputes within our representative institutions. But this capacity does not always come easily. Students must learn how to frame their disputes and discussions in such a way that they can acquire enlightened beliefs while also questioning others in a manner that upholds civility. Famous Americans, both living and dead, have given voice to the prominence of this habit. Thomas Jefferson stated in his first inaugural address (as cited in Library of Congress, n.d.), "Every difference of opinion is not a difference of principle." President Barack Obama famously observed when announcing his candidacy for the presidency (as cited in "Barack Obama's Campaign Speech," 2007) that we can "disagree without being disagreeable."

   And as Westheimer (2017) explains:
   > Although most of us would agree that traditions are important, without questioning there can be no progress. Dissent—feared and suppressed in nondemocratic societies—is the engine of progress in free ones. Education reformers, school leaders, and parents should do everything possible to ensure that teachers and students have opportunities to ask these kinds of questions.

When schools and teachers model this behavior better than the general public, it has two benefits: (1) in the short term, it improves public perception of schools, and (2) in the long run, it fosters hope of creating meaningful accords of progress both in the public square and within our institutions of government.

2. **Seek respectful conversations from multiple perspectives:** In 2017, I published an open letter to the class of 2018 in the *HuffPost* in which I explain what bothers me most about 21st century political discourse:

> The tone, tenor, and pitch of our civic discourse has devolved into a monotonous carousal of shrill invective and tired outrage, a never-ending news cycle that feeds itself on a vapid and corrosive tribalism in which there is no hope of ever reaching consensus or compromise. American politics has morphed into a tragi-comedy in which the proliferation of impersonal social media platforms amplifies voices of outrageous indignation or ad hominem attacks. Virtual town squares result in an endless stream of digital cut and thrust where the aim is not mutual understanding or meaningful accords of recognition but complete annihilation of those we disagree with. (Adams, 2017)

Many of the democratic ailments I identify can be counteracted by encouraging students to approach an issue from multiple perspectives. You can nurture this healthy, productive civic habit in virtually any subject and in all grade levels. An English teacher might ask students, "What are different interpretations of this poem?" A government or environmental-science teacher might ask, "Why would a carbon tax be a good idea, or who might it harm?" A history or biology instructor might ask, "Why do certain people have strong objections to specific scientific theories?"

Respectful dialogue and discussion help relax tension. They also aid in the formation of wise public policy and demonstrate to students that conducting the business of a diverse nation does not require vitriol or contempt. Repairing the fissure between the public and its schools will require respectful conversations between educators and the broader public. Thus, when communities have a better understanding of these difficulties, it can positively affect everything from funding and recruitment to curriculum and disciplinary policies.

3. **Root instruction in local contexts:** While national politics grabs many headlines and certainly is the subject of endless chatter in journalistic circles and on social media platforms, local government actually makes the most

difference in teachers' and students' lives. This is why, instead of having students talk, write, debate, or read about issues of national importance, teachers should orient instruction around issues that students are certain to encounter in their daily lives. Every community faces endless decisions about how best to govern itself. From building roads to electing mayors, there are plenty of issues from which you can create lessons and encourage democratic habits. As Westheimer (2017) argues, "Schools should encourage students to consider their specific surroundings and circumstances. It's not possible to teach democratic forms of thinking without providing an environment to think about."

This approach encourages young people to come into contact with the people and institutions making important decisions in their communities. Again, when average U.S. citizens interact with students and schools in their own communities, their impressions of students and educators are generally positive. To this end, a great way to ease tensions between teachers and their communities is to have communities observe the products of their schools. This is more likely to occur if instruction is rooted in local issues and concerns.

Summary

Reflecting on the relationship between schools and communities raises a number of pivotal questions: What does it mean to be a good community member? What does it mean to be a good citizen? Most of all, what does it mean to be a good teacher within the community in which one teaches? How we answer these questions will go a long way in helping us understand our roles and responsibilities as citizen-educators.

The tension between teachers and the public can seem insurmountable at times. Fortunately, teachers can ease this tension by working assiduously to highlight their and their students' successes. The need to highlight positive news and contributions is especially great in an era in which media outlets put special emphasis on failure and dysfunction. Teachers can also build bridges by bringing community members and former students into learning communities. Having members of the outside community observe and participate in educational activities not only gives students a valuable resource but also will likely improve community members' impressions of a school's quality. Finally, teachers themselves can improve relationships with the community by modeling the virtues of high-minded, civil, democratic discourse.

RIDE *the* WAVE

STRATEGY 3

In the spirit of respecting and understanding different perspectives, fill in the following chart, which concerns controversial or timely topics in education. Use a brief sentence to explain your perspective on each of the following educational issues. Then attempt to articulate why those who disagree with you believe what they do. Students can, of course, engage in the same activity, with the teacher replacing issues of education with any controversial or debatable topics.

Issue	My View	Opposing View
Charter schools		
Merit pay for teachers		
Standardized testing		
Teacher tenure		
Other		

Visit **go.SolutionTree.com/teacherefficacy** *for a free reproducible version of this feature box.*

Democracy requires strong institutions and asks much of its citizens. Democracies all over the world, and especially in North America, emphasize that political legitimacy rests on the shoulders of the body politic—that government is not the sovereign of the people but an instrument for protecting the rights and freedoms of the people, the demos, so that they may live individual lives as they see fit. If there is one thread of truth that does not change in the long course of political history, it is this: democracy does not work when schools do not succeed. To this end, we must take mindful steps to repair the chasm between the public and its schools in order to ensure the nation's success.

EPILOGUE

Character is destiny.
— HERACLITUS

For the first time in my adult life, I couldn't control the tears. Not even a little.

My sudden loss of control disoriented me. I didn't feel like myself. The world suddenly pulsed with sorrow in a way I had only read about in books or seen in movies. I had known loss before. I had known heartbreak. But this was something foreign, something so overwhelming and soulfully tragic it became impossible for me to process or explain. I didn't need a scientist or a priest to explain this surge of fury—I needed a poet.

I sat on an airplane heading east for my twentieth college reunion with a blank legal pad in front of me, consumed by the tragedy that had occurred just two days earlier. My tears flowed seemingly in infinite supply. The man next to me had to ask me if something was wrong. I knew what I had to do, knew what I had to write, knew what awaited me when I returned home in just a few days. For the first time in my life, I was going to have to deliver a eulogy—a eulogy I'd never imagined I would have to compose or deliver.

My friend of twenty-five years and my closest colleague had suddenly and unexpectedly died of cancer just four weeks after her fortieth birthday. She had been my partner in coaching the speech-and-debate team when we were in our early twenties, my collaborator in teaching Advanced Placement courses to high school seniors for fifteen years (she taught AP literature, I taught AP government), and my neighbor just down the hallway for nineteen years. The doctors had misdiagnosed her condition as neurofibromatosis type 2, a rare disorder that involves noncancerous tumors, which gave the cancer months to ravage her body.

She died on a Tuesday, but it was Wednesday that tested my resolve as a man and as a teacher. That was a day like no other, a day for which there was no lesson plan, no workshop to draw on, no running away. On Tuesday afternoon, the principal had gotten on the school's PA system and told my friend's students—almost all of whom were also my students—to immediately gather in the school's auditorium, where he eventually announced her death to them. Only a few of her friends on campus had known how grave her condition had become. Tragically, some students later told me they had thought the announcement was going to include her triumphantly walking onto the stage in a grand return to teaching. After the principal's announcement, my task on Wednesday was to stand in front of four different periods of students and explain to them what had happened to my dear friend and their extraordinary teacher.

I write these very words just two days short of the first anniversary of her death. There is not a day, or even a class period, that goes by when I do not think of her or miss her. For months after her passing, when I heard news or gossip, I would pick up my phone to text her. I refused to walk down to her side of the hall for weeks. For almost two decades, I'd talked to her about virtually every significant issue that came up in my classes. We had talked about our students, our calendars, and our lives outside the classroom. I had sought her input or approval for virtually every teaching idea I'd had. She certainly would have read this entire book and offered her constructive feedback. But now she is gone, and the conclusion of her life has become the inspiration for the conclusion of this book.

I write about her death because this is a book about learning how to thrive as a teacher in an environment of constant, and sometimes difficult, change. The loss of my friend was yet one more change I had to absorb, an immensely personal one that affected my life both in and out of the classroom. As I sat on that plane after her death, it occurred to me that teaching without her would be like a two-engine airplane trying to maintain altitude when one of its engines has stopped working. It just didn't feel possible. Learning how to teach without my dear friend has been one of the hardest changes I have ever had to endure.

When I began my career in the late 1990s, no one had conversations about a need to confront constant change or the varying tensions change perpetuates in our professional lives. In the teaching profession, we never know what will come around the next corner—what will accompany any shift in the culture or in broader society. We never know how the students will change, how the laws will change, and what role we will have amid these mountains of change. But this much is certain: teachers want to be able to handle whatever comes their way with grace, professionalism, and an appetite to make a difference in the lives of the students in their classrooms.

It is true that change is perhaps the one constant of life. Even the ancient Greeks realized this two millennia ago and based much of their moral philosophy on this facet of the human experience. In the teaching profession, change can be scary, it can be fast, and it often makes demands of us we don't immediately welcome. But this is no reason to lose the potency of our optimism as educators. Of all the skills the next generation of teachers should hope to acquire, knowing how to absorb these worries without creating tension in the different relationships that define the education profession is perhaps the key for civility to reign and progress to materialize far into the 21st century.

As teachers, we owe it to ourselves to repair the defining relationships of our profession and do everything we can do to restore the hope, optimism, and inspiration that led most of us to the classroom in the first place. As citizens, we owe it to our communities to remain vigilant against the temptations to become negative, to abandon foundational relationships, or to turn a diffident eye to the next wave of reform. As human beings, we cannot maintain hope without also believing that better days are yet to come. It is my honest and sober ambition that this book will help usher in these better days. I hope it can help educators across the country confront the challenges that are certain to come their way. Teachers, of all people, can change the direction and tone of civil society because we know that what makes the world a better place is not *the world* recognizing teachers but *teachers* recognizing what the world needs and springing into action to meet those needs.

This book represents my own modest springing into action. The outcomes I wish to encourage and the professional flourishing I hope to inspire stand as totems in a professional sea of modern frustration and confusion. I hope these ambitions come to fruition—not for myself and not only for teachers but for our children, who need the adults in their lives to clear away the shrubbery of an intimidating world.

We can do it. But we need one another—we need strong relationships. We need to repair the ruptures and mitigate the schisms present in our professional lives. We need to believe anew in the promise of education.

REFERENCES *and* RESOURCES

Adams, J. S. (2012). *Full classrooms, empty selves: Reflections on a decade of teaching in an American high school.* Scotts Valley, CA: CreateSpace.

Adams, J. S. (2014, November 25). *The magical solution illusion: How everyone has "the answer" to education.* Accessed at https://theeducatorsroom.com/magical-solution-illusion-everyone-answer-education on July 17, 2019.

Adams, J. S. (2016). *The secrets of timeless teachers: Instruction that works in every generation.* Lanham, MD: Rowman & Littlefield.

Adams, J. S. (2017, August 28). Dear class of 2018: For democracy to survive, we must learn to talk to one other again. *HuffPost.* Accessed at www.huffpost.com/entry/dear-class-of-2018-for-democracy-to-survive-we-must_b_59a4badae4b03c5da162af18 on July 17, 2019.

Adams, J. S. (2018, April 16). *10 things teachers DID NOT have to deal with 10 years ago.* Accessed at https://theeducatorsroom.com/10-things-teachers-did-not-have-to-deal-with-10-years-ago on July 17, 2019.

Allen, J. (2015, June 8). *When teachers compete, no one wins* [Blog post]. Accessed at www.edutopia.org/blog/when-teachers-compete-janet-allen on July 17, 2019.

American Federation of Teachers. (2017). *2017 educator quality of work life survey.* Accessed at www.aft.org/sites/default/files/2017_eqwl_survey_web.pdf on August 21, 2019.

American Heritage dictionary of the English language (3rd ed.). (1992). Boston: Houghton Mifflin Harcourt.

American School Counselor Association. (n.d.). *Helping kids after a shooting.* Accessed at www.schoolcounselor.org/school-counselors/professional-development/learn-more/shooting-resources on July 17, 2019.

American University's School of Education. (2019, March 10). *The current state of teacher burnout in America* [Blog post]. Accessed at https://soeonline.american.edu/blog/the-current-state-of-teacher-burnout-in-america on November 13, 2019.

Apps announced at Apple's Chicago education event. (2018, March 27). Accessed at www.cnet.com/pictures/all-the-2018-education-apps-apple-announced/ on November 16, 2019.

Austin, V., Shah, S., & Muncer, S. (2005). Teacher stress and coping strategies used to reduce stress. *Occupational Therapy International, 12*(2), 63–80. Accessed at www.onlinelibrary.wiley.com/doi/pdf/10.1002/oti.16 on July 17, 2019.

Baeder, J. (2012, October 22). Why U.S. schools are simply the best [Blog post]. *Education Week.* Accessed at https://blogs.edweek.org/edweek/on_performance/2012/10/why_us_schools_are_simply_the_best.html on July 17, 2019.

Barack Obama's campaign speech. (2007, February 10). *The Guardian.* Accessed at www.theguardian.com/world/2007/feb/10/barackobama on November 22, 2019.

Battelle for Kids. (2011). *Successfully implementing transformational change in education: Lessons learned about the importance of effective change leadership and strategic communications.* Accessed at www2.ed.gov/programs/racetothetop/communities/bfk-rttt-communications-lessons-learned.pdf on July 17, 2019.

Billett, P., Burns, E., & Fogelgarn, R. (2019, May 5). *Almost every Australian teacher has been bullied by students or their parents, and it's taking a toll.* Accessed at https://theconversation.com/almost-every-australian-teacher-has-been-bullied-by-students-or-their-parents-and-its-taking-a-toll-116058 on November 22, 2019.

Boogren, T. H. (2018). *Take time for you: Self-care action plans for educators.* Bloomington, IN: Solution Tree Press.

Bosso, D. (2017, May). *Teacher morale, motivation, and professional identity: Insight for educational policymakers from State Teachers of the Year.* Accessed at https://files.eric.ed.gov/fulltext/ED581425.pdf on November 12, 2019.

Bowler, K. (2018). *Everything happens for a reason: And other lies I've loved.* New York: Random House.

Bridges, W. (2009). *Managing transitions: Making the most of change* (3rd ed.). Philadelphia: Da Capo Press.

Burton, T. (2015). *Exploring the impact of teacher collaboration on teacher learning and development* (Doctoral dissertation). University of South Carolina, Columbia. Accessed at https://scholarcommons.sc.edu/cgi/viewcontent.cgi?article=4103&context=etd on November 17, 2019.

Catapano, J. (n.d.). *Relationship building with teacher colleagues.* Accessed at www.teachhub.com/relationship-building-teacher-colleagues on July 17, 2019.

Centers for Disease Control and Prevention. (2016). *QuickStats: Death rates for motor vehicle traffic injury, suicide, and homicide among children and adolescents aged 10–14 years—United States, 1999–2014.* Accessed at http://dx.doi.org/10.15585/mmwr.mm6543a8 on August 22, 2019.

Child Mind Institute. (n.d.). *Going back to school after a tragedy.* Accessed at https://childmind.org/article/going-back-school-tragedy on July 17, 2019.

Clare, H. (2017). *Icebreaker: A voyage far north.* London: Chatto & Windus.

Cohen, D. B. (2016). *Capturing the spark: Inspired teaching, thriving schools*. Palo Alto, CA: Enactive.

Cohen, D. B. (2017). Managing change—before it drives you out of teaching. *Educational Leadership, 74*(9), 34–38.

Cox, J. (n.d.). *Dealing with unsupportive colleagues in the teaching profession*. Accessed at www.teachhub.com/dealing-unsupportive-colleagues-teaching-profession on July 17, 2019.

Cox, J. W., Rich, S., Chiu, A., Muyskens, J., & Ulmanu, M. (2018, May 8). Database: How many children have experienced school shootings in America? *The Washington Post*. Accessed at www.washingtonpost.com/graphics/2018/local/school-shootings-database/ on September 4, 2019.

Daniels, L. A. (1988, September 14). Study shows teachers still feel left out on policy. *The New York Times*. Accessed at www.nytimes.com/1988/09/14/us/education-study-shows-teachers-still-feel-left-out-on-policy.html on July 17, 2019.

Davila, J., Hershenberg, R., Feinstein, B. A., Gorman, K., Bhatia, V., & Starr, L. R. (2012). Frequency and quality of social networking among young adults: Associations with depressive symptoms, rumination, and corumination. *Psychology of Popular Media Culture, 1*(2), 72–86.

Davis, J. (2015, September 14). Give teachers time to collaborate. *Education Week*. Accessed at www.edweek.org/ew/articles/2015/09/16/give-teachers-time-to-collaborate.html on July 17, 2019.

De La Rosa, S. (2018, March 16). *Schools sharing success over social media*. Accessed at https://districtadministration.com/schools-sharing-success-over-social-media on July 17, 2019.

Denby, D. (2016, February 23). Do teens read seriously anymore? *The New Yorker*. Accessed at www.newyorker.com/culture/cultural-comment/books-smell-like-old-people-the-decline-of-teen-reading on November 13, 2019.

Diliberti, M., Jackson, M., & Kemp, J. (2017). *Crime, violence, discipline, and safety in U.S. public schools: Findings from the School Survey on Crime and Safety: 2015–16* (NCES 2017–122). Accessed at https://nces.ed.gov/pubs2017/2017122.pdf on August 22, 2019.

Donovan, S. R. (2014, December). *Learning from academically optimistic teachers: Supporting teacher academic optimism* (Doctoral thesis). Northeastern University, Boston. Accessed at https://repository.library.northeastern.edu/files/neu:349613/fulltext.pdf on September 5, 2019.

Doyle, M., & Burton, G. (2018, January 17). The school principal as change agent [Blog post]. *Education Week*. Accessed at https://blogs.edweek.org/edweek/next_gen_learning/2018/01/the_school_principal_as_change_agent.html on July 17, 2019.

DuFour, R., & Fullan, M. (2013). *Cultures built to last: Systemic PLCs at Work*. Bloomington, IN: Solution Tree Press.

DuFour, R., & Mattos, M. (2013). How do principals really improve schools? *Educational Leadership, 70*(7), 34–40. Accessed at www.ascd.org/publications/educational-leadership/apr13/vol70/num07/How-Do-Principals-Really-Improve-Schools%C2%A2.aspx on July 17, 2019.

Dwyer, R. J., Kushlev, K., & Dunn, E. W. (2018). Smartphone use undermines enjoyment of face-to-face social interactions. *Journal of Experimental Social Psychology, 78*, 233–239.

Eaker, R., & Keating, J. (2009, July 22). *Team leaders in a professional learning community* [Blog post]. Accessed at www.allthingsplc.info/blog/view/54/team-leaders-in-a-professional-learning-community on July 17, 2019.

Edgerson, D. E., Kritsonis, W. A., & Herrington, D. (2006). The critical role of the teacher-principal relationship in the improvement of student achievement in public schools of the United States. *The Lamar University Electronic Journal of Student Research, 3*. Accessed at https://files.eric.ed.gov/fulltext/ED491985.pdf on July 17, 2019.

Eller, J. F., & Eller, S. A. (2013). Working with difficult staff. *Educational Leadership, 70*(7). Accessed at www.ascd.org/publications/educational-leadership/apr13/vol70/num07/Working-with-Difficult-Staff.aspx on July 17, 2019.

Engel, P. (Producer). (1989). *Saved by the bell* [Television series]. New York: NBC.

Feltoe, G. (2015, September 22). *Sources of teacher stress*. Accessed at www.teachermagazine.com.au/articles/sources-of-teacher-stress on November 21, 2019.

Ferguson, M. (2018). *Public opinion on teachers and teaching*. Accessed at http://pdkpoll.org/perspectives/washington-view-public-opinion-on-teachers-and-teaching on July 17, 2019.

Ferlazzo, L. (2018, June 12). Response: Too many professional development "horror stories" [Blog post]. *Education Week*. Accessed at https://blogs.edweek.org/teachers/classroom_qa_with_larry_ferlazzo/2018/06/response_too_many_professional_development_horror_stories.html on July 17, 2019.

Figlio, D. N. (2005, March). *Testing, crime and punishment* (Working Paper No. 11194). Cambridge, MA: National Bureau of Economic Research. Accessed at www.nber.org/papers/w11194 on July 17, 2019.

Fullan, M. (2001). *The new meaning of educational change* (3rd ed.). New York: Teachers College Press.

Gallup. (n.d.a). *Confidence in institutions*. Accessed at https://news.gallup.com/poll/1597/confidence-institutions.aspx on August 22, 2019.

Gallup. (n.d.b). *Congress and the public*. Accessed at https://news.gallup.com/poll/1600/congress-public.aspx on August 22, 2019.

Garcia, E. (2015, August 11). *When teachers compete with other teachers* [Blog post]. Accessed at https://educationtothecore.com/2015/08/when-teachers-compete-with-other-teachers on July 17, 2019.

Gardner, M., Roth, J., & Brooks-Gunn, J. (2008). Adolescents' participation in organized activities and developmental success 2 and 8 years after high school: Do sponsorship, duration, and intensity matter? *Developmental Psychology, 44*(3), 814–830. Accessed at http://citeseerx.ist.psu.edu/viewdoc/download?doi=10.1.1.579.7597&rep=rep1&type=pdf on November 21, 2019.

Garrison Institute. (2009, April 10). *Garrison Institute's CARE program for teachers receives federal funding* [Press release]. Accessed at www.garrisoninstitute.org/wp-content/uploads/2015/10/Garrison_Institute_IES_grant_10Apr09.pdf on July 18, 2019.

Gill, B. (2017, April 13). *Redefining accountability to treat teachers and leaders like the professionals they are* [Blog post]. Accessed at www.brookings.edu/blog/brown-center-chalkboard/2017/04/13/redefining-accountability-to-treat-teachers-and-leaders-like-the-professionals-they-are on July 17, 2019.

Glatter, H., DeRuy, E., & Wong, A. (2016, September 4). The failing grade for tests. *The Atlantic*. Accessed at www.theatlantic.com/education/archive/2016/09/the-failing-grade-for-tests/498407 on July 17, 2019.

Goldstein, D. (2014). *The teacher wars: A history of America's most embattled profession*. New York: Doubleday.

Gonzalez, J. (2017, June 19). *Why it's so hard for teachers to take care of themselves (and 4 ways to start)* [Blog post]. Accessed at www.cultofpedagogy.com/teacher-self-care on July 17, 2019.

Gooley, J. J., Chamberlain, K., Smith, K. A., Khalsa, S. B. S., Rajaratnam, S. M. W., Van Reen, E., et al. (2011). Exposure to room light before bedtime suppresses melatonin onset and shortens melatonin duration in humans. *Journal of Clinical Endocrinology and Metabolism, 96*(3), E463–E472.

Graf, N. (2018, April 18). *A majority of U.S. teens fear a shooting could happen at their school, and most parents share their concern*. Accessed at www.pewresearch.org/fact-tank/2018/04/18/a-majority-of-u-s-teens-fear-a-shooting-could-happen-at-their-school-and-most-parents-share-their-concern on July 17, 2019.

Grafwallner, P. (2017, October 16). *Coaching the veteran teacher*. Accessed at www.edutopia.org/article/coaching-veteran-teacher on July 17, 2019.

Graham, E. (n.d.). *Using smartphones in the classroom*. Accessed at www.nea.org/tools/56274.htm on July 17, 2019.

Granata, K. (2014). Teacher stress and disengagement impacts student performance. *Education World*. Accessed at www.educationworld.com/a_curr/teacher-stress-impacts-student-performance.shtml on November 4, 2019.

Gray, J. A., & Summers, R. (2015). International professional learning communities: The role of enabling school structures, trust, and collective efficacy. *International Education Journal: Comparative Perspectives, 14*(3), 61–75. Accessed at https://files.eric.ed.gov/fulltext/EJ1086795.pdf on January 2, 2020.

Grissom, J. A., Kalogrides, D., & Loeb, S. (2017). Strategic staffing? How performance pressures affect the distribution of teachers within schools and resulting student achievement. *American Educational Research Journal, 54*(6), 1079–1116. Accessed at https://journals.sagepub.com/doi/abs/10.3102/0002831217716301 on July 17, 2019.

Hampson, R. (2019, April 8). We followed 15 of America's teachers on a day of frustrations, pressures and hard-earned victories. *USA Today.* Accessed at www.usatodaycom/in-depth/news/nation/2018/10/17/teachers-appreciation-pay-union-jobs-schools-education/1509500002 on July 17, 2019.

Hargreaves, A., & Fullan, M. (2012). *Professional capital: Transforming teaching in every school.* New York: Teachers College Press.

Hartz, A. M. (2018, May). *Teacher perceptions of school gun violence* (Doctoral dissertation). Temple University, Philadelphia. Accessed at https://digital.library.temple.edu/digital/collection/p245801coll10/id/500938 on September 5, 2019.

Hefling, K., & Doherty, T. (2018, March 1). *Trump sees veterans as the perfect armed teachers, but they're divided.* Accessed at www.politico.com/story/2018/03/01/trump-armed-teachers-veterans-373732 on November 16, 2019.

Herman, K. C., Hickmon-Rosa, J., & Reinke, W. M. (2018). Empirically derived profiles of teacher stress, burnout, self-efficacy, and coping and associated student outcomes. *Journal of Positive Behavior Interventions, 20*(2), 90–100.

Hirsh-Pasek, K., Zosh, J. M., Golinkoff, R. M., Gray, J. H., Robb, M. B., & Kaufman, J. (2015). Putting education in "educational" apps: Lessons from the science of learning. *Psychological Science in the Public Interest, 16*(1), 3–34. Accessed at https://journals.sagepub.com/stoken/rbtfl/GxHiSvddIDi.E/full on July 17, 2019.

Ingersoll, R. M. (2012, May 16). Beginning teacher induction: What the data tell us. *Education Week.* Accessed at www.edweek.org/ew/articles/2012/05/16/kappan_ingersoll.h31.html on July 17, 2019.

Interlandi, J. (2018, September 5). Teaching in the age of school shootings. *The New York Times Magazine.* Accessed at www.nytimes.com/interactive/2018/09/05/magazine/school-shootings-teachers-support-armed.html on July 17, 2019.

Jennings, J. L., & Bearak, J. M. (2014). "Teaching to the test" in the NCLB era: How test predictability affects our understanding of student performance. *Educational Researcher, 43*(8), 381–389. Accessed at https://journals.sagepub.com/doi/abs/10.3102/0013189x14554449 on July 17, 2019.

Johnson, M. (2015, November 4). *The online lives of Canadian youth.* Accessed at https://vanierinstitute.ca/online-lives-canadian-youth/?unapproved=5772&moderation-hash=52235e32ed06fd2a5a2cee2432fef5cd#comment-5772 on January 2, 2020.

Jones, W. M., & Dexter, S. (2014). How teachers learn: The roles of formal, informal, and independent learning. *Educational Technology Research and Development, 62*(3), 367–384. Accessed at https://link.springer.com/article/10.1007%2Fs11423-014-9337-6 on July 17, 2019.

Jung, L. A. (2017). How to keep mutiny from sinking your change effort. *Educational Leadership, 74*(9), 28–32. Accessed at www.ascd.org/publications/educational-leadership/jun17/vol74/num09/How-to-Keep-Mutiny-from-Sinking-Your-Change-Effort.aspx on July 17, 2019.

K–12 Education Team. (2015). *Teachers know best: Teachers' views on professional development*. Seattle, WA: Bill & Melinda Gates Foundation. Accessed at http://k12education.gatesfoundation.org/resource/teachers-know-best-teachers-views-on-professional-development on July 17, 2019.

Kaplan, C., Chan, R., Farbman, D. A., & Novoryta, A. (2015). *Time for teachers: Leveraging expanded time to strengthen instruction and empower teachers*. Boston: National Center on Time and Learning. Accessed at https://files.eric.ed.gov/fulltext/ED561995.pdf on July 17, 2019.

Kemp, S. (2019, January). *Digital in 2019*. Accessed at https://wearesocial.com/global-digital-report-2019 on December 31, 2019.

Klassen, R. M., & Chiu, M. M. (2010). Effects on teachers' self-efficacy and job satisfaction: Teacher gender, years of experience, and job stress. *Journal of Educational Psychology, 102*(3), 741–756.

Krammer, M., Rossmann, P., Gastager, A., & Gasteiger-Klicpera, B. (2018). Ways of composing teaching teams and their impact on teachers' perceptions about collaboration. *European Journal of Teacher Education, 41*(4), 463–478. Accessed at www.tandfonline.com/doi/full/10.1080/02619768.2018.1462331 on July 17, 2019.

Kriegel, O. (n.d.). *How to move past a conflict with your school principal*. Accessed at www.wgu.edu/heyteach/article/how-move-past-conflict-your-school-principal1802.html on July 17, 2019.

Kuhn, J. (2013, December 26). *The exhaustion of the American teacher*. Accessed at https://theeducatorsroom.com/the-exhaustion-of-the-american-teacher on July 17, 2019.

Kumar, S. (2017). New generation teacher: Roles and responsibilities. *Indian Journal of Health and Wellbeing, 8*(8), 817–818. Accessed at http://iahrw.com/article.php?numb=1&article=YXVGVTVhQUNCVUZDdm1xYjM2K0NBQT09 on July 17, 2019.

Laderas-Kilkenny, N. (2007, August 15). *Professional jealousy among educators* [Blog post]. Accessed at https://nkilkenny.wordpress.com/2007/08/15/professional-jealousy-among-educators on July 17, 2019.

Lamb-Sinclair, A. (2018, February 22). Teaching while afraid. *The Atlantic*. Accessed at www.theatlantic.com/education/archive/2018/02/teaching-while-afraid/553931 on July 17, 2019.

Lander, J. (2016, December 20). *Students as teachers: Exploring the mutual benefits of peer-to-peer teaching—and strategies to encourage it* [Blog post]. Accessed at www.gse.harvard.edu/uk/blog/students-teachers on July 17, 2019.

Lawless, B. (2017, October 31). *The many hats of the teacher* [Blog post]. Accessed at https://lawlesslearning.com/2017/10/31/the-many-hats-of-the-teacher on July 17, 2019.

Leiter, M. P., & Maslach, C. (1998). Burnout. In H. S. Friedman (Ed.), *Encyclopedia of mental health* (Vol. 1, pp. 347–357). San Diego, CA: Academic Press.

Lenhart, A. (2015, April 9). *Teens, social media and technology overview 2015*. Washington, DC: Pew Research Center. Accessed at www.pewresearch.org/wp-content/uploads/sites/9/2015/04/PI_TeensandTech_Update2015_0409151.pdf on July 17, 2019.

Lenzini, A. (2018, April 12). *The many roles of a teacher* [Blog post]. Accessed at https://publish.illinois.edu/uistudteachaml/2018/04/12/the-many-roles-of-a-teacher on July 17, 2019.

Library of Congress. (n.d.). *Creating the United States: Peaceful transition*. Accessed at www.loc.gov/exhibits/creating-the-united-states/peaceful-transition.html on January 4, 2020.

Loewenstein, S. (2014, January 20). *The accidental community: Feeling the love* [Blog post]. Accessed at www.edutopia.org/blog/accidental-community-feeling-the-love-shira-loewenstein on July 17, 2019.

Long, C. (2012, November 26). *How blaming teachers shortchanges students*. Accessed at http://neatoday.org/2012/11/26/how-blaming-teachers-shortchanges-students-2/ on December 31, 2019.

Matthews, D. (2018, October 30). *Billionaires are spending their fortunes reshaping America's schools. It isn't working.* Accessed at www.vox.com/future-perfect/2018/10/30/17862050/education-policy-charity on November 11, 2019.

McComb, S. (2014, September 25). Teaching students, not subjects: Why we need a deeper learning approach. *HuffPost*. Accessed at www.huffpost.com/entry/teaching-students-not-sub_b_5883986 on July 17, 2019.

McCoy, B. (2013). Digital distractions in the classroom: Student classroom use of digital devices for non-class related purposes. *Faculty Publications, College of Journalism & Mass Communications, 71*. Accessed at https://digitalcommons.unl.edu/cgi/viewcontent.cgi?article=1070&context=journalismfacpub on July 17, 2019.

McIlheran, J. (2018, August 8). Veteran teachers: It's our responsibility to support new colleagues. *Education Week Teacher*. Accessed at www.edweek.org/tm/articles/2018/08/08/veteran-teachers-its-our-responsibility-to-support.html on July 17, 2019.

Meador, D. (2018, July 9). *The importance of effective communication between teachers*. Accessed at www.thoughtco.com/the-importance-of-effective-teacher-to-teacher-communication-3194691 on July 17, 2019.

Meikle, J. (2012, February 3). Twitter is harder to resist than cigarettes and alcohol, study finds. *The Guardian*. Accessed at www.theguardian.com/technology/2012/feb/03/twitter-resist-cigarettes-alcohol-study on August 21, 2019.

Mental Health America. (n.d.a). *Tips for teachers: Ways to help students who struggle with emotions or behavior*. Accessed at www.mhanational.org/tips-teachers-ways-help-students-who-struggle-emotions-or-behavior on September 5, 2019.

Mental Health America. (n.d.b). *Who we are*. Accessed at www.mhanational.org/who-we-are on September 5, 2019.

Mercado, M. C., Holland, K., Leemis, R. W., Stone, D. M., & Wang, J. (2017, November 21). Trends in emergency department visits for nonfatal self-inflicted injuries among youth aged 10 to 24 years in the United States, 2001–2015. *JAMA, 318*(19), 1931–1933. Accessed at https://jamanetwork.com/journals/jama/fullarticle/2664031 on July 17, 2019.

MetLife. (2012, March). *The MetLife survey of the American teacher: Teachers, parents and the economy.* New York: Author. Accessed at https://files.eric.ed.gov/fulltext/ED530021.pdf on August 21, 2019.

Moir, E., Barlin, D., Gless, J., & Miles, J. (2009). *New teacher mentoring: Hopes and promise for improving teacher effectiveness.* Cambridge, MA: Harvard Education Press.

Montgomery, C., & Rupp, A. A. (2005). A meta-analysis for exploring the diverse causes and effects of stress in teachers. *Canadian Journal of Education, 28*(3), 458–486.

Mosle, S. (2014, September). Building better teachers. *The Atlantic.* Accessed at www.theatlantic.com/magazine/archive/2014/09/building-better-teachers/375066 on July 17, 2019.

National Alliance on Mental Illness. (2019). *Mental health by the numbers.* Accessed at www.nami.org/learn-more/mental-health-by-the-numbers on July 17, 2019.

National Center on Education and the Economy. (n.d.). *Finland: Teacher and principal quality.* Accessed at http://ncee.org/what-we-do/center-on-international-education-benchmarking/top-performing-countries/finland-overview/finland-teacher-and-principal-quality/ on November 22, 2019.

National Child Traumatic Stress Network. (2008, October). *Child trauma toolkit for educators.* Los Angeles: National Center for Child Traumatic Stress.

National Council of Teachers of English. (2014). *How standardized tests shape—and limit—student learning.* Urbana, IL: Author. Accessed at www.ncte.org/library/NCTEFiles/Resources/Journals/CC/0242-nov2014/CC0242PolicyStandardized.pdf on July 17, 2019.

National Education Association. (2015). *ESEA reauthorization: Excessive high-stakes testing has negative effects on students, teachers.* Accessed at www.nea.org/assets/docs/TestingMemberSurvey(RES)0215.pdf on July 17, 2019.

National Institute of Mental Health. (2017). *Major depression.* Accessed at www.nimh.nih.gov/health/statistics/major-depression.shtml#part_155032 on August 21, 2019.

National Sleep Foundation. (n.d.). *Challenging ways technology affects your sleep.* Accessed at www.sleep.org/articles/ways-technology-affects-sleep/ on January 2, 2020.

Neighmond, P. (2019, March 14). *A rise in depression among teens and young adults could be linked to social media use.* Accessed at www.npr.org/sections/health-shots/2019/03/14/703170892/a-rise-in-depression-among-teens-and-young-adults-could-be-linked-to-social-medi on November 15, 2019.

Nguyen, T. (2017, December). *America's youth is in crisis—Here's how you can help* [Blog post]. Accessed at www.mhanational.org/blog/americas-youth-crisis-heres-how-you-can-help on September 5, 2019.

Nichols, S. (2018). *Why teachers are walking out.* Accessed at www.scarymommy.com/why-teachers-are-walking-out on July 17, 2019.

Nielsen. (2017, February 28). *Mobile kids: The parent, the child and the smartphone.* Accessed at www.nielsen.com/us/en/insights/news/2017/mobile-kids-the-parent-the-child-and-the-smartphone.html on July 17, 2019.

Office of Population Affairs. (2016, October 28). *A picture of adolescent health.* Accessed at www.hhs.gov/ash/oah/facts-and-stats/picture-of-adolescent-health/index.html on August 27, 2019.

Office of Population Affairs. (2018, July 17). *A day in the life of a high school teen.* Accessed at www.hhs.gov/ash/oah/facts-and-stats/day-in-the-life/index.html on August 27, 2019.

Office of Population Affairs. (2019, February 25). *Adolescent mental health basics.* Accessed at www.hhs.gov/ash/oah/adolescent-development/mental-health/adolescent-mental-health-basics/index.html on August 21, 2019.

O'Hara, M. (2018, July 31). Young people's mental health is a "worsening crisis." Action is needed. *The Guardian.* Accessed at www.theguardian.com/society/2018/jul/31/young-people-mental-health-crisis-uk-us-suicide on July 17, 2019.

O'Keefe, B. (2011, October 19). *5 steps to better school/community collaboration: Simple ideas for creating a stronger network* [Blog post]. Accessed at www.edutopia.org/blog/school-community-collaboration-brendan-okeefe on July 17, 2019.

OpenSecrets. (n.d.). *Reelection rates over the years.* Accessed at www.opensecrets.org/overview/reelect.php on August 22, 2019.

Oplatka, I. (2006). Teachers' perceptions of their role in educational marketing: Insights from the case of Edmonton, Alberta. *Canadian Journal of Educational Administration and Policy, 51.* Accessed at https://files.eric.ed.gov/fulltext/EJ843437.pdf on July 17, 2019.

Ortiz, S. P. (2006, May 10). National teacher day. *Congressional Record, 152*(56), E769. Accessed at www.congress.gov/crec/2006/05/10/CREC-2006-05-10-pt1-PgE769.pdf on August 22, 2019.

Overman, S. (n.d.). *Fighting the stress of teaching to the test.* Accessed at www.nea.org/tools/fighting-stress-teaching-to-Test.html on July 17, 2019.

Phi Delta Kappan. (2018, September). *The 50th annual PDK poll of the public's attitudes toward the public schools.* Arlington, VA: Author. Accessed at http://pdkpoll.org/assets/downloads/pdkpoll50_2018.pdf on July 17, 2019.

Potash, B. (2018, August 16). *Teachers, we need to do our own PR to advocate for ourselves and our kids.* Accessed at www.weareteachers.com/teacher-pr on July 17, 2019.

Powell, A. (2009). *The cornerstone: Classroom management that makes teaching more effective, efficient, and enjoyable.* Due Season Press.

Pro Essay Writer. (n.d.). *Modern teachers and their duties* [Blog post]. Accessed at https://pro-essay-writer.com/blog/teacher-quality on July 17, 2019.

Psychology Today. (n.d.). *Find a therapist.* Accessed at www.psychologytoday.com/intl/counsellors?domain=www&cc=us&cl=en on December 31, 2019.

Putnam, R. D. (2000). *Bowling alone: The collapse and revival of American community.* New York: Simon & Schuster.

Ravitch, D. (2016, July 23). The Common Core costs billions and hurts students. *The New York Times*. Accessed at www.nytimes.com/2016/07/24/opinion/sunday/the-common-core-costs-billions-and-hurts-students.html on July 17, 2019.

Reeves, D. B. (2010). *Transforming professional development into student results*. Alexandria, VA: Association for Supervision and Curriculum Development.

Resnick, B. (2019, May 16). Have smartphones really destroyed a generation? We don't know. *Vox*. Accessed at www.vox.com/science-and-health/2019/2/20/18210498/smartphones-tech-social-media-teens-depression-anxiety-research on November 5, 2019.

Rieg, S. A., & Marcoline, J. F. (2008, February). *Relationship building: The first "R" for principals*. Paper presented at the Eastern Educational Research Association Conference, Hilton Head, SC.

Ripley, A. (2013a). *The smartest kids in the world: And how they got that way*. New York: Simon & Schuster.

Ripley, A. (2013b, October). The case against high-school sports. *The Atlantic*. Accessed at www.theatlantic.com/magazine/archive/2013/10/the-case-against-high-school-sports/309447/ on November 21, 2019.

Ronfeldt, M., Farmer, S. O., McQueen, K., & Grissom, J. A. (2015, June). Teacher collaboration in instructional teams and student achievement. *American Educational Research Journal, 52*(3), 475–514. Accessed at https://doi.org/10.3102/0002831215585562 on August 22, 2019.

Rousmaniere, K. (2013, November 8). The principal: The most misunderstood person in all of education. *The Atlantic*. Accessed at www.theatlantic.com/education/archive/2013/11/the-principal-the-most-misunderstood-person-in-all-of-education/281223 on July 17, 2019.

Sands, G. (2017, January 4). Are the PISA education results rigged? *Forbes*. Accessed at www.forbes.com/sites/realspin/2017/01/04/are-the-pisa-education-results-rigged/#36dfe8c71561 on July 17, 2019.

Santoro, D. A. (2018). *Demoralized: Why teachers leave the profession they love and how they can stay*. Cambridge, MA: Harvard Education Press.

Schneider, J. (2017, July 17). Why Americans think so poorly of the country's schools. *The Atlantic*. Accessed at www.theatlantic.com/education/archive/2017/07/the-education-perception-gap/533898 on July 17, 2019.

Schneider, J., Jacobsen, R., White, R. S., & Gehlbach, H. (2018). The (mis)measure of schools: How data affect stakeholder knowledge and perceptions of quality. *Teachers College Record, 120*(6), 1–40.

Schrage, M. (2012, December 13). A simpler way to get employees to share. *Harvard Business Review*. Accessed at https://hbr.org/2012/12/a-simpler-way-to-get-employees-to-share.html on July 17, 2019.

Schwarzer, R., & Hallum, S. (2008). Perceived teacher self-efficacy as a predictor of job stress and burnout: Mediation analyses. *Applied Psychology, 57*(1), 152–171.

Seneca, L. A. (2016). *Seneca's letters from a Stoic* (R. M. Gummere, Trans.). Mineola, NY: Dover Publications. (Original work published 1918).

Shafer, L. (2017, December 15). *Social media and teen anxiety.* Accessed at www.gse.harvard.edu/news/uk/17/12/social-media-and-teen-anxiety on August 21, 2019.

Shafer, L. (2018, July 23). *What makes a good school culture?* Accessed at www.gse.harvard.edu/news/uk/18/07/what-makes-good-school-culture on July 17, 2019.

Shaked, H., & Schechter, C. (2017). School principals as mediating agents in education reforms. *School Leadership and Management, 37*(1), 19–37. Accessed at https://doi.org/10.1080/13632434.2016.1209182 on July 17, 2019.

Shulman, L. S. (2004). *The wisdom of practice: Essays on teaching, learning, and learning to teach* (S. M. Wilson, Ed.). San Francisco: Jossey-Bass.

Shulman, R. D. (2019). *The number 1 meditation app is now free for teachers and their students.* Accessed at www.forbes.com/sites/robynshulman/2019/02/25/the-number-1-meditation-app-is-now-free-for-teachers-and-their-students/#4dfbcb8a7d47 on November 16, 2019.

Skaalvik, E. M., & Skaalvik, S. (2007). Dimensions of teacher self-efficacy and relations with strain factors, perceived collective teacher efficacy, and teacher burnout. *Journal of Educational Psychology, 99*(3), 611–625.

Sorkin, A. (Writer), & Glatter, L. L. (Director). (2003). Inauguration: Over there [Television series episode]. In A. Sorkin (Executive producer), *The West Wing*. New York: National Broadcasting Company.

Southern Regional Education Board. (2018, January). *Educator effectiveness: Mentoring new teachers.* Accessed at www.sreb.org/sites/main/files/file-attachments/mentoring_new_teachers_2.pdf on July 17, 2019.

Stapleton, P. (2019, June 6). Teachers are more depressed and anxious than the average Australian. Accessed at https://theconversation.com/teachers-are-more-depressed-and-anxious-than-the-average-australian-117267 on November 22, 2019.

Steele, W. (Ed.). (2017). *Optimizing learning outcomes: Proven brain-centric, trauma-sensitive practices.* New York: Routledge.

Stone, D. (1996). *I'd rather see a sermon: Showing your friends the way to heaven.* Joplin, MO: College Press.

Strauss, V. (2015, August 24). The real reasons behind the US teacher shortage. *The Washington Post.* Accessed at www.washingtonpost.com/news/answer-sheet/wp/2015/08/24/the-real-reasons-behind-the-u-s-teacher-shortage on July 17, 2019.

Strauss, V. (2016, December 23). Teacher: A one-size-fits-all approach to instruction is stifling our classrooms. *The Washington Post.* Accessed at www.washingtonpost.com/news/answer-sheet/wp/2016/12/23/teacher-a-one-size-fits-all-approach-to-instruction-is-stifling-our-classrooms/?utm_term=.4cef53e8b375 on July 17, 2019.

Strauss, V. (2018, April 18). Ten problems teachers did not have to deal with a decade ago. *The Washington Post.* Accessed at www.washingtonpost.com/news/answer-sheet/wp/2018/04/18/ten-problems-teachers-did-not-have-to-deal-with-a-decade-ago on August 21, 2019.

Sullivan, A. (2016, September 19). I used to be a human being. *New York Magazine.* Accessed at http://nymag.com/intelligencer/2016/09/andrew-sullivan-my-distraction-sickness-and-yours.html on July 17, 2019.

Swartzer, K. (2018, February 28). *The causes of teacher burnout: What everyone needs to know* [Blog post]. Accessed at www.learnersedge.com/blog/causes-of-teacher-burnout on July 17, 2019.

Team Clarizen. (2018, June 21). Five things to know about the bottom up strategy [Blog post]. *Clarizen.* Accessed at www.clarizen.com/fivethings-to-know-about-the-bottom-up-strategy/ on November 19, 2019.

Teng, M. F. (2017). Emotional development and construction of teacher identity: Narrative interactions about the pre-service teachers' practicum experiences. *Australian Journal of Teacher Education, 42*(11), 117–134. Accessed at https://files.eric.ed.gov/fulltext/EJ1161164.pdf on August 21, 2019.

Terhart, E. (2013). Teacher resistance against school reform: Reflecting an inconvenient truth. *School Leadership and Management, 33*(5), 486–500. Accessed at https://doi.org/10.1080/13632434.2013.793494 on July 17, 2019.

Thiers, N. (2017). Making progress possible: A conversation with Michael Fullan. *Educational Leadership, 74*(9), 8–14. Accessed at www.ascd.org/publications/educational-leadership/jun17/vol74/num09/Making-Progress-Possible@-A-Conversation-with-Michael-Fullan.aspx on July 17, 2019.

Thompson, D. (2010, December 28). U.S. education is much better than you think. *The Atlantic.* Accessed at www.theatlantic.com/business/archive/2010/12/us-education-is-much-better-than-you-think/68635 on July 17, 2019.

TNTP. (2013). *Perspectives of irreplaceable teachers: What America's best teachers think about teaching.* New York: Author. Accessed at https://tntp.org/assets/documents/TNTP_Perspectives_2013.pdf on July 17, 2019.

Tromholt, M. (2016). The Facebook experiment: Quitting Facebook leads to higher levels of well-being. *Cyberpsychology, Behavior, and Social Networking, 19*(11), 661–666.

Trosclair, A. (2015, January 27). *Why a teacher cannot have a normal life . . .* Accessed at https://theeducatorsroom.com/teacher-cannot-normal-life on July 17, 2019.

Twenge, J. M. (2017a). *iGen: Why today's super-connected kids are growing up less rebellious, more tolerant, less happy—and completely unprepared for adulthood—and what that means for the rest of us.* New York: Atria Books.

Twenge, J. M. (2017b, September). Have smartphones destroyed a generation? *The Atlantic.* Accessed at www.theatlantic.com/magazine/archive/2017/09/has-the-smartphone-destroyed-a-generation/534198 on July 17, 2019.

Urban, H. (2008). *Lessons from the classroom: 20 things good teachers do*. Redwood City, CA: Great Lessons Press.

Van Beck, S. (2011). *The importance of the relationships between teachers and school principals* (Unpublished doctoral dissertation). University of Houston. Accessed at https://uh-ir.tdl.org/handle/10657/258 on July 17, 2019.

Vanderhye, R. (2015). 3 essentials to motivate and retain veteran teachers. *Principal*, *94*(4), 40–41. Accessed at www.naesp.org/sites/default/files/Vanderhye_MA15.pdf on July 17, 2019.

Venables, D. R. (2011). *The practice of authentic PLCs: A guide to effective teacher teams*. Thousand Oaks, CA: Corwin Press.

Vescio, V., Ross, D., & Adams, A. (2008). A review of research on the impact of professional learning communities on teaching practice and student learning. *Teaching and Teacher Education*, *24*(1), 80–91. Accessed at www.sciencedirect.com/science/article/pii/S0742051X07000066 on July 17, 2019.

Walker, T. (2018, January 18). *Teacher burnout or demoralization? What's the difference and why it matters*. Accessed at http://neatoday.org/2018/01/18/teacher-burnout-disillusionment on July 17, 2019.

Walker, T. (2019, October 18). *"I didn't know it had a name": Secondary traumatic stress and educators*. Accessed at http://neatoday.org/2019/10/18/secondary-traumatic-stress/ on November 12, 2019.

Ward, S. C. (2015, April 10). Why has teacher morale plummeted? *Newsweek*. Accessed at www.newsweek.com/why-has-teacher-morale-plummeted-321447 on July 17, 2019.

Westheimer, J. (2017). What kind of citizens do we need? *Educational Leadership*, *75*(3), 12–18. Accessed at www.ascd.org/publications/educational-leadership/nov17/vol75/num03/What-Kind-of-Citizens-Do-We-Need%C2%A2.aspx on July 17, 2019.

Whitebook, M., & Bellm, D. (2014, July/August). Mentors as teachers, learners, and leaders. *Exchange*, *218*, 14–18. Accessed at https://cscce.berkeley.edu/files/2014/FINAL-218-Whitebook-Bellm1.pdf on July 17, 2019.

Wyman, K. (2017, March 22). *5 ways to involve the community in your classroom*. Accessed at https://education.cu-portland.edu/blog/classroom-resources/involve-community-classroom on July 17, 2019.

Zarra, E. J., III. (2013). *Teacher-student relationships: Crossing into the emotional, physical, and sexual realms*. Lanham, MD: Rowman & Littlefield.

Zarra, E. J., III. (2018). *The teacher exodus: Reversing the trend and keeping teachers in the classrooms*. Lanham, MD: Rowman & Littlefield.

Zimmerman, J. (2006, September). Why some teachers resist change and what principals can do about it. *NASSP Bulletin*, *90*(3), 238–249. Accessed at https://pdfs.semanticscholar.org/64de/3b75717b98785ad057e69b573f538b566ae3.pdf on July 17, 2019.

INDEX

A

accepting change, 119
accountability
    sparking jealousies, 74, 79–81
active coping, 27–29
Adams, H., 3–4
administration, 5–6, 103–104, 128–129
    avoiding stereotypes, 126–128
    employing empathy, 126–128
    facing resistance, 111–112
    feedback and reflection, 120–123
    flourishing, 7
    identifying divergent perspectives, 105–106
    local and global responsibilities, 108–111
    power games, 117–120
    powerlessness, 106–108
    threats to professional climate, 113–115
    transforming through transparency, 123–126
    turnover, 86
Allen, J., 80–81
alumni in the classroom, 148–149
American Federation of Teachers, 16
American Heritage Dictionary, 126
American School Counselor Association, 65
American University's School of Education, 17–18
apps, 58
    Calm, 61
    Atlantic, 67, 110
Aurora (Colo.) Public Schools, 91

Austin, V., 30
avoiding fiefdoms, 95

B

bad press, 136–139
    myth of systemic failure, 139–141
Banales, F., 49
Barlin, D., 89
Battelle for Kids, 120
Bearak, J. M., 48
Bellm, D., 90
Billett, P., 136–137
body politic
    creating, 85–88
Boogren, T. H., 14–15
Bosso, D., 15
bottom-up collaboration, 96–99
Bowler, K., 74
Bowling Alone (Putnam), 84
Bridges, W., 123, 125
Brooks-Gunn, J., 138
Brown v. Board of Education, 137
burnout, 17–19
Burns, E., 136–137
Burton, G., 106–107
Burton, T., 75

C

Capturing the Spark (Cohen), 4
Carlston Family Foundation, 145
Catapano, J., 95
cell phones, 2, 43–45
    effects on mental health, 46–47
    in the classroom, 55–59

Centers for Disease Control and Prevention, 45–46
Chan, R., 76
changes in education
    adapting to, 3–4
    recognizing, 2–3
Child Mind Institute, 67
Chiu, A., 49–50
Chiu, M., 17
Clare, H., 3
class size, 16
Cohen, D. B., 4, 119
collaboration
    being there for each other, 95–96
    bottom-up, 96–99
    building, 74–87
    committing to, 85, 99–101
    creating a body politic, 85–88
    seeking mentors and mentees, 89–91
    sharing ideas, 91–94
colleagues, 5–6, 71–72
    being there for each other, 95–96
    bottom-up collaboration, 96–99
    building collaboration, 74–77
    committing to collaboration, 85, 99–101
    conflict resolution, 73–74
    creating a body politic, 85–88
    friends and, 82–84, 120
    generational chasms, 78–79
    jealousies and juxtapositions, 79–81
    nominating for recognition, 145
    seeking mentors and mentees, 89–91
    sharing ideas, 91–94
    supporting, 95–96
Collier County Public Schools (Fla.), 144
Columbine High School shootings, 50
Common Core, 48
communication
    between colleagues, 85–88, 91–94
    expectations, 128
    feeling ignored, 111–112, 134–136
    hurt feelings, 111–112
    negative language, 113–115
    sharing ideas, 91–94
    staff cohesion and, 117–129
    two-way, 120–123
community, 5–6, 131–132
    bad press, 136–139
    connecting to schools, 143
    demonstrating democracy, 150–155
    highlighting successes, 143–146
    involving in lessons, 147–148
    myth of systemic failure, 139–141
    pressures and frustrations, 134–136
    remembering school, 147–150
    viewing education from a distance, 133–134
compassion, 62
    beyond the classroom, 106–108
    fatigue, 24–27
conflict resolution, 73–74
coping
    good vs. bad, 27–29
    strategies in the classroom, 59–62
The Cornerstone (Powell), 62
Cox, J. W., 49–50, 81
Cult of Pedagogy (Gonzalez), 19–20
Cultures Built to Last (DuFour & Fullan), 77

D

Davis, J., 16, 76
defining success, 53–54
De La Rosa, S., 144
demonstrating democracy, 150–154
Demoralized (Santoro), 3
Denby, D., 44
depersonalization, 18–19
Diliberti, M., 67
Doherty, T., 67
Donovan, S. R., 34–35
Doyle, M., 106–107
DuFour, R., 77
Dunn, E., 47
Dwyer, R., 47

E

Eaker, R., 83
Edgerson, D., 126

Education Week, 76, 106–107, 137
Educational Leadership (Westheimer), 152
Educator's Room, 2
educator vs. teacher, 95–96
Eller, J., 113
Eller, S., 113
embarrassment, 61–62
emotional exhaustion, 18–19
empathy, 87
    among staff, 126–128
    beyond the classroom, 106–108
    vs. sympathy, 126
Every Student Succeeds Act, 140
expectations, 40–42
    communicating, 128
experienced teachers, 6
    as mentors, 89–91

F

Facebook, 144–145
Farbman, D. A., 76
Farmer, S. O., 75
fear of missing out, 44
feedback, 120–123
feeling ignored, 111–112, 134–136
"Fighting the Stress of Teaching to the Test" (Overman), 49
Figlio, D., 48–49
Finnish schools, 77
flourishing, 6–8
Fogelgarn, R., 136–137
friendship, 128
    developing, 98
    vs. colleagues, 82–84
Fristad, M., 47
Fullan, M., 77, 93

G

Gardner, M., 138
Gastager, A., 96
Gasteiger-Klicpera, B., 96
Gehlbach, H., 140
general criticizers, 113–114
Gill, B., 82–83
Gless, J., 89

Global Teacher Prize, 145
goal setting, 29–32
Goldstein, D., 15
Gonzalez, J., 19–20
gossip, 86
Graf, N., 50
Grafwallner, P., 78
Granata, K., 19
Gray, J. A., 72
Grissom, J., 48, 75
Guest, E. A., 98
gun violence, 49–51
    community differences, 67–68
    honest dialogue, 65, 67
    planning for, 65–67
    reassuring students, 67

H

Halla, K., 57–58
Hallum, S., 18–19
happiness, 86
Hargreaves, A., 93
Hartz, A. M., 50
Harvard Business Review, 93
Hefling, K., 67
Herman, K., 20
Herrington, D., 126
Hickmon-Rosa, J., 20
highlighting successes, 143–146
high-stakes testing, 2, 17–18
    creating jealousies, 80
    differences between countries, 137–138
    effects on students, 47–49
    relaxing, 62–65
Hirsh-Pasek, K., 58
Holland, K., 46
House of Cards, 130
HuffPost, 153
humility, 86
hurt feelings, 111–112

I

Icebreaker (Clare), 3
Instagram, 144
Interlandi, J., 50–51

island teachers, 114
isolation, 26, 74–84
"I Used to Be a Human Being" (Sullivan), 43

J

Jackson, M., 67
Jacobsen, R., 140
jealousies, 74, 79–81
Jefferson, T., 152
Jennings, J., 48
Jennings, P., 15
Johnson, M., 44
Jung, L. A., 111–112

K

Kalogrides, D., 48
Kaplan, C., 76
Keating, J., 83
Kemp, J., 67
Kemp, S., 43
kids before content, 53–55
kindness, 86
Klassen, R., 17
Krammer, M., 96
Kriegel, O., 119
Kritsonis, W. A., 126
Kuhn, J., 3
Kumar, S., 41
Kumashiro, K. K., 40
Kushlev, K., 47

L

Laderas-Kilkenny, N., 80
Lamb-Sinclair, A., 67
Lander, J., 148
Leemis, R. W., 46
Lenhart, A., 44
Levitt, T., 61
local vs. global responsibilities, 108–111
Loeb, S., 48

M

Managing Transitions (Bridges), 123
Marcoline, J., 120
Matthews, D., 8

McComb, S., 53
McCoy, B., 57
McQueen, K., 75
Meador, D., 86, 88
Meikle, J., 45
Mental Health America, 45, 59
mental-health issues, 45–47
mentoring, 89–91
Mercado, M. C., 46
The MetLife Survey of the American Teacher, 16–17
Miles, J., 89
Milken Educator Awards, 145
The (Mis)measure of Schools (Schneider et al.), 140
Moir, E., 89
Montgomery, C., 27–29
Mosle, S., 76
Muncer, S., 30
mutual accountability, 83
Muyskens, J., 49–50
myth of systemic failure, 139–141

N

National Alliance on Mental Illness, 45
National Center on Education and the Economy, 77
National Child Traumatic Stress Network, 26–27
National Council of Teachers of English, 48
National Education Association, 82
National Institute of Mental Health, 46
National Sleep Foundation, 45
National Survey on Drug Use and Health, 46
National Teacher of the Year Program, 145
National Teachers Hall of Fame, 145
NEA Foundation Awards for Teaching Excellence, 145
negative language, 113–115
Neighmond, P., 46–47
New Republic, 43
Newsweek, 15
new teachers, 7
    as mentees, 89–91
New York Times, 16

New York Times Magazine, 50–51
Nguyen, T., 45
Nichols, S., 3
No Child Left Behind, 48, 108
Novoryta, A., 76

O

Obama, B., 152
O'Hara, M., 46
O'Keefe, B., 150
on-the-job retirees, 113
open-mindedness, 87
Oplatka, I., 81
optimism, 32–35
Ortiz, S., 119
Overman, S., 49

P

pacified teaching, 65–68
parents
    lack of support from, 2, 32, 37–38, 40–42
    working with, 62
Parkland school shootings, 50, 67
passive coping, 27
Pay, 17, 32
Pearson National Teaching Awards, 145
Pew Research Center, 44, 50
political environments, 17
Potash, B., 145
poverty, 2
Powell, A., 62, 64
power games, 117–120
powerlessness, 106–108
praise, 61, 87
"The Principal" (Rousmaniere), 110–111
problem solving, 125–126
Professional Capital (Hargreaves & Fullan), 93
professional climate
    threats to, 113–115
professional development, 122–123
    generational chasms in, 78–79
professional learning communities, 73, 75
promoting learning
    pacified teaching, 65–68
    standardized testing, 62–65

    teaching students, not subjects, 53–55
    using coping strategies, 59–62
    using technology, 55–59
Psychology Today, 27
Putnam, R., 84
"Putting Education in 'Educational' Apps" (Hirsh-Pasek et al.), 58

Q

Quinn, P., 137–138

R

Race to the Top, 48, 108
Ravitch, D., 48
reduced personal accomplishments, 18–19
reflection, 120–123
Reinke, W., 20
"Relationship Building With Teacher Colleagues" (Catapano), 95
relationships, 8–9
    repairing, 158–159
    strengthening, 4–6
    student-teacher, 56, 65
    teacher-administrator, 105–115
remind, 57
resistance, 106–108, 111–112
Resnick, B., 46
resources
    lack of, 17
respect, 126–128, 153
    lack of, 134–136
Rich, S., 49–50
Rieg, S., 120
Ripley, A., 138
Ronfeldt, M., 75
Rossmann, P., 96
Roth, J., 138
Rousmaniere, K., 110–111
Rupp, A., 27–29

S

Sands, G., 137
Sandy Hook Elementary School shootings, 50
Santoro, 3
Schechter, C., 105

Schneider, J., 139–140
school safety
    bullying of teachers, 16, 136–137
    community differences, 67–68
    gun violence, 49–51, 65–68
    have a plan, 65–67
    honest dialogue, 65, 67
    reassuring students, 67
    threats to, 2
Schrage, M., 93
Schwarzer, R., 18–19
Scott, L. H., 117–118
self, 5–6, 11–12, 20–21
    21st century toll on, 14–17
    caring for, 13–14, 19–20
    teacher stress, 17–19
self-care, 13–14
    benefits of, 19–20
    strategies, 23–36
self-reflection, 29–32
Seneca, 68
sense of control, 23–24
"Sermons We See" (Guest), 98
Shafer, L., 43, 118
Shah, S., 30
Shaked, H., 105
sharing ideas, 91–94
sharing success, 123
Shulman, L., 42, 51
Shulman, R. D., 61
Skaalvik, E. M., 17
Skaalvik, S., 17
social media, 43–45
    in the classroom, 55–59
    creating jealousies, 80
    effects on mental health, 46–47
    using to highlight successes, 143–145
social support services, 16
staff cohesion, 117–129
Stapleton, P., 137
stay yourself, 23–24
Steele, W., 20
stereotypes
    avoiding, 126–128
Stone, D. M., 46
stress
    good vs. bad coping, 27–29
    reducing, 59–61
    students, 37–51
    teachers, 17–19, 79–81
students, 5–6, 37–38
    accommodating, 61
    anxiety, 2
    high-stakes testing, 47–49
    involving in collaboration, 99
    involving in school promotion, 145
    lack of parental support, 40–42
    mental health issues, 45–47, 59
    mitigating anxiety, 53–68
    proliferating platforms, 43–45
    school violence, 49–51
    stress, 39–40
    supporting, 54
    taking into the community, 149–150
student-teacher interactions, 56
    honest dialogue, 65
suicide, 46
Sullivan, A., 43
Summers, R., 72
support, 54
supporting colleagues, 95–96

T

Take Time for You (Boogren), 14–15
taking the initiative, 98
teacher-administrator dynamics, 105–115
The Teacher Exodus (Zarra), 3
teachers
    being bullied, 16, 136–137
    being there for each other, 95–96
    benefits of self-care, 19–20
    bottom-up collaboration, 96–99
    building collaboration, 74–77
    burnout, 17–19
    committing to collaboration, 85, 99–101
    conflict resolution, 73–74
    creating a body politic, 85–88
    divergent principal perspectives, 105–115
    expanding expectations on, 40–42
    experienced vs. new, 6–7, 78–79

friends vs. colleagues, 82–84
generational chasms, 78–79
good vs. bad coping, 27–29
jealousies and juxtapositions, 79–81
leaders, 7–8
pacified teaching, 65–68
pressures and frustrations, 134–136
resistance to change, 106–108, 111–112
seeking mentors and mentees, 89–91
sharing ideas, 91–94
stress, 17–19, 79–81
student mental health and, 45–47
teacher-to-teacher communication, 85–88
The Teacher Wars (Goldstein), 15
"Teaching While Afraid" (Lamb-Sinclair), 67
teach students, not subjects, 53–55
Team Clarizen, 99
technology
    finding the golden mean, 55–59
    out of date, 16
Teng, M. F., 23–24
Terhart, E., 108
"Thief of the Month," 93
Thiers, N., 125
thinking local, 98–99
TNTP, 54
Toner, P., 135
transparency, 123–126
Tromholt, M., 47
Trosclair, A., 3
Trump, D. J., 67
trust, 87, 126–128
Twenge, J. M., 43–44, 47
Twitter, 57, 144
2018 Phi Delta Kappan poll, 135

U

U.S. Dept. of Health and Human Services Office of Population Affairs, 45–46
Ulmanu, M., 49–50
underminers, 113
USA Today, 134–135
"Using Smartphones in the Classroom" (Graham), 57

V

Van Beck, S., 126–128
Vanderhye, R., 79
Vanier Institute of the Family, 44
viewing education from a distance, 133–134
    bad press, 136–139
    myth of systemic failure, 139–141
    pressures and frustrations, 134–136
Virginia Tech shootings, 50

W

Walker, 3
Wang, J., 46
Ward, S. C., 15
Washington Post, 50, 135
    Answer Sheet, 2
Westheimer, J., 152, 154
The West Wing, 130
"We Wuz Robbed," 93
"When Teachers Compete, No One Wins" (Allen), 80–81
White, R. S., 140
Whitebook, M., 90
Wyman, K., 147–148

Y

YouTube, 145

Z

Zarra, E. J., 3, 58

180 Days of Self-Care for Busy Educators
Tina H. Boogren
Rely on *180 Days of Self-Care for Busy Educators* to help you lead a happier, healthier, more fulfilled life inside and outside of the classroom. With Tina H. Boogren's guidance, you will work through 36 weeks of self-care strategies during the school year.
BKF920

Take Time for You
Tina H. Boogren
The key to thriving as a human and an educator rests in self-care. With *Take Time for You*, you'll discover a clear path to well-being. The author offers manageable strategies, reflection questions, and surveys that will guide you in developing an individualized self-care plan.
BKF813

HEART!
Timothy D. Kanold
Explore the concept of a heartprint—the distinctive impression an educator's heart leaves on students and colleagues during his or her professional career. Use this resource to reflect on your professional journey and discover how to increase efficacy, and foster productive, heart-centered classrooms and schools.
BKF749

Finding Fulfillment
Robin Noble
Develop a renewed sense of well-being, satisfaction, and happiness in your career. Designed for teachers and administrators, *Finding Fulfillment* outlines how to develop processes and best practices that impact not only your students' growth but also your growth as an educator and change-maker.
BKF893

Solution Tree | Press

Visit SolutionTree.com or call 800.733.6786 to order.

"Tremendous, tremendous, tremendous!

The speaker made me do some very deep internal reflection about the **PLC process** and the personal responsibility I have in making the school improvement process work for **ALL kids**."

—Marc Rodriguez, teacher effectiveness coach,
Denver Public Schools, Colorado

PD Services

Our experts draw from decades of research and their own experiences to bring you practical strategies for building and sustaining a high-performing PLC. You can choose from a range of customizable services, from a one-day overview to a multiyear process.

Book your PLC PD today!
888.763.9045

Solution Tree